The Conversation Series

The
Conversation
Series 27

Matthew Barney

Hans Ulrich Obrist

Verlag der Buchhandlung Walther König

I

Beginnings and Endings with Jonathan Bepler, 2001

Hans Ulrich Obrist | So Matthew, let's begin with the beginnings. Your work suddenly became visible with two exhibitions in 1991. Could you tell me about this and how it all started in the 1980s?

Matthew Barney | In my mind, the work from that period had more to do with live performance, even if those exhibitions were understood more as video installations. The videos had an agenda of documenting real-time action. And right around that time, in '91, I started to become interested in telling stories rather than telling the truth of documenting real-time action. So, in a certain way, that was a real turning point for me, rather than a beginning. Although they were my first exhibitions, maybe it was the end of something, as much as the beginning of something else.

HUO | Could you tell me about this more performative period when you were interested in real-time performances?

MB | I was developing environments that would impose a resistance on pretty straightforward activities that I would perform, to see how that would affect the forms that were created in the environment. There was a series of pieces called *Drawing Restraint,* and those environments were about imposing resistance on the act of drawing. In a certain way those pieces in the two gallery exhibitions in '91 were related to the *Drawing Restraints*, in the way that the protagonist climbed across the ceiling and marked up the ceiling with his shoes. This was definitely a continuation of the *Drawing Restraint* project in the way that an athletic language was used, where training devices from American Football, like blocking sleds for example, would be pushed across the floor with drawing implements attached to make marks in unpredictable ways on the floor. Blocking sleds and weight training equipment became emblematic as creative tools, in spite of the fact they were designed to break down the muscles of the athlete using them. I was attracted to the physiology of the athletic body, and the way that muscles depend on resistance in order to gain strength and mass. A lot of the work around that time was focused on the metaphor that a form could not really grow without resistance. And in that way a lot of the athletic systems that I have grown up with became really useful as models, and as starting points for the story I was interested in telling.

HUO | And that was when you were at art school, or was it before?

MB | That was at art school.

HUO | All of a sudden these things that were familiar to you entered the work. There are two issues that crop up really, really early in your work and have been referred to as childhood obsessions of yours: Jim Otto and Houdini. Can you tell me about the beginnings of Otto and Houdini?

MB | Houdini eventually became something else for me, for sure. But I think this interest in the beginning had to do with this idea of his taking on resistance as a choice . . . a self-imposed resistance, with a creative potential. And this tended to ignore the fact that Houdini was a showman. It was more about the way Houdini learned the devices of restraint so thoroughly that his escape became an intuitive practice. A police force would be invited to put him in a straitjacket, and to lock him with any type of lock they chose. Sometimes they even designed a lock just for the occasion. He so thoroughly understood every lock design of the time, that he had a pick for every possible lock combination, hidden away somewhere in his body. His was a very physical and highly intuitive practice within the realm of magic and illusion, and that interested me a lot. Jim Otto ended up being a kind of analogue to that in some ways. Otto was a quintessential, over-determined competitor. He never missed a football game in his career, though he played with an absurd number of leg injuries and endured knee replacements in the off-season. He would play injured, essentially. He was a masochist. He was known as a kind of iron man. Nothing could stop him. He was an excellent player. I guess there was also that: I needed at that point to find a character who could define the difference between the field of competition and the field of preparation, where potential energy is developed and stored. Otto is interesting in that way because he was a center. The center puts the ball into play. Once he moves the ball, the competition starts, and the potential energy is spent. So in this narrative, you can imagine Houdini as the quarterback who is expected to receive the ball from Otto. Otto wants to get the game started, but Houdini is resistant. Houdini wants to save the potential energy he has accumulated, while Otto is willing to spend it all in the name of competition.

HUO | When you mentioned constraint before, I was wondering if there was also a kind of oscillation between constraint and escape. Is this somehow related to the Houdini issue?

MB | Yes, Houdini was very much on my mind when those pieces were being made, for sure.

HUO | The *Drawing Restraint* series started very early and then went on for many years in a similar way to *Cremaster.* Before talking about *Cremaster,* can you talk about the evolution of the *Drawing Restraint* series?

MB | There were a number of them made before '91 that were similar in their intentions. And those were all trials. Environments were set up in the studio to challenge the act of drawing in a very direct way. Then, *Drawing Restraint 7* [1993] was made a couple of years later, after my interest had moved a little bit more towards narrative. Within the story of *Drawing Restraint 7*, there are three satyrs. There is one who drives the vehicle.

HUO | Which is you!

MB | Which is me, yes, and that character just chases his tail endlessly. And there are two satyrs in the back of the vehicle, which is a limousine, who are collaborating in some way. One is using various wrestling holds on the other, to control his head. And with the controlled head, using the satyr's horn as a drawing tool, he is trying to make a drawing in the sunroof where condensation was building up. The limousine attempts to cross the bridges and tunnels into Manhattan, but fails to enter. With each attempt to enter, the drawing erases itself, so they have to start over again. Although this deals with some of the same ideas as the early *Drawing Restraints, Drawing Restraint 7* took a very different approach. In fact, the project may have had more to do with placing a resistance on theatrical delivery. As the work became more narrative, I got interested in how an actor could be involved in the work without performing in a mannered way. Putting the actor in prosthetics, and in this case adding another joint to the legs of the satyrs was part of this experiment. That, in combination with placing them in a claustrophobic environment in the back of the limousine. Although the situation was very theatrical, there was very little acting happening. They were just trying to remain balanced, and carry out a sequence of movements. That experiment ended up informing a lot of the characters in the *Cremaster* series.

HUO | In *Drawing Restraint 7*, for the first time in your work, like later on in *Cremaster*, one can find more links in terms of mythology. How did this emerge in your work?

MB | It started in the project that preceded *Drawing Restraint 7*, which was *OTTOshaft* [1992]. *OTTOshaft* was a story that took place in the parking garage and the various elevator shafts within the museums at *documenta IX*. Using these different locations, a bagpipe was suggested. The parking garage became the bag, and the elevator shafts became the drones. Although it wasn't my initial intention, *OTTOshaft* stared to feel something like the myth of Pan and Echo, in the way that the pipers started to look like fauns running through a forest, which was the parking garage. Several known myths started to come forward in an unexpected way, which I found exciting. I became interested in the idea that the project could live inside a known story, and still remain abstract. Not so different from the way the *Cremaster* pieces align themselves with a cinematic genre and use the genre to transform into something else. It interested me to see how far the project could travel into existing worlds, and still come back to a more abstract place in the end.

Jonathan Bepler | I have a question on objects. In a way, the impulse to edit is kind of like making the performance into an object, and also the object as a piece of sculpture. I think there are two layers of that in the films, where the actors themselves are just objects, and the whole thing is kind of a piece of sculpture, maybe more than a film. When I was thinking of the earlier stuff, the question was that you were making an object, a drawing in that sense. Did you exhibit that at that time? When did you start exhibiting objects in addition to the film or video objects?

MB | The *Drawing Restraint* pieces were definitely not about making finished works. It had more to do with the apparatus, or the system that made it . . . some kind of meditative process. I guess something changed when the emphasis on storytelling shifted, and it felt more useful to make distillations of the narrative into objects to make the piece clear.

HUO | Throughout the 1990s the object was often described as a trigger for something else, or an excuse. Is this a valid definition for you?

MB | In those earlier projects, the apparatus always came first, and from there everything else followed. That happens occasionally now, but more often, it is the opposite: the narrative falls into place and the object follows. But I think in either case they are both very necessary for me to complete the story.

HUO | How did *Cremaster* start, and when did you give it the name?

MB | *Cremaster* actually started with the *OTTOshaft* project. *OTTOshaft* fractured a narrative into a number of different locations, and then brought it back together as one form. The *Cremaster* idea started as a literal extension of *OTTOshaft*, where five locations could be assigned to the mouthpiece, the chanter, and the bass and tenor drones of the bagpipe. Around that time, I started talking to James Lingwood about making a project in the United Kingdom. I was interested in having one of the five locations in Celtic territory. I ended up traveling around the Isle of Man. Things fell into place in that year.

HUO | Under which circumstances was the title given?

MB | Looking back at the early *Drawing Restraints*, there was a system that I laid out at that time as a way of mapping my creative process. The system started in a space called "Situation," which was a sexual place, where drive or desire would initiate the creative impulse. The impulse would then pass through a visceral space that would funnel, and shape that raw drive. That space was called "Condition." The third space, called "Production," was the anal or oral output, where the initial impulse would take its final form. I was interested in the idea of bypassing "Production," by connecting those two orifices and making a circular system. "Situation" was always represented by a drawing of a reproductive system before the point of sexual differentiation in a developing fetus. In that stage, the internal sexual organs sit higher in the body, before they drop into their male or female position. [*pause*] I was at a wedding; my sister's wedding, sitting next to a doctor, who I grew up with in Idaho. Dr. Lung was his name. I was talking to Dr. Lung about using this undifferentiated stage in sexual development as part of this larger metaphorical system, and I told him that I was interested in framing it in a more narrative way, and he said I should really look at the cremaster muscle. He suggested that, within the fantasy I was starting to describe, the cremaster muscle could move the reproductive system up and down, switching between male and female, at will.

HUO | And was it already clear at that time that *Cremaster* would become a whole series?

MB | It began as five locations. Two of them were changed slightly. The Isle of Man started out as a location in Ireland, and then that was adjusted. And *Cremaster 2* [1999] changed twice. Originally it was Columbia Icefields, and then it switched to the White Sands desert, and then it went back to the Columbia Icefields. The other three locations were fixed, and did not change.

JB | How long did you figure it would take?

MB | A lot less time than it did. At that time the projects I was making would take about six months, so I thought I could do it in a couple years.

JB | Yes, your mind has been on that Lung idea for a couple of years. [*laughs*]

HUO | I think Richard Flood said you did it like George Lukas. Was this something you had in mind?

MB | I started in the Isle of Man first [*Cremaster 4*, 1994], simply because I was approached by an English curator to work in an unspecified place in that area, and by doing that first, I enjoyed the fact that the narratives would not fall together in a linear fashion. After that, I made *Cremaster 1* [1995], in some way to establish a kind of boundary. *Cremaster 5* [1997] came next . . . the other boundary. Around that time I felt pretty certain that ending in the middle would be the right way to finish.

HUO | Sylvère Lotringer writes about the function violence assumes in sadomasochism, which is not a fictitious exercise in private fetishism, but a highly realistic form of social therapy.[1] And that is something we could inject into the path we were following before.

MB | I think the way the body was used in these projects had more to do with an understanding I had of my own body, and not necessarily the way that I relate to other people's bodies. The meaning, for me, grew out of my experience as an athlete.

1 Neville Wakefield and Richard Flood, *Matthew Barney: Pace Car for the Hubris Pill* (Rotterdam: Museum Boijmans Van Beuningen, 1995).

HUO | Can you tell me about your practice as an athlete?

MB | It was something that I grew up with. I competed in football and Greco-Roman wrestling . . . I suppose these are the two sports that have been most useful to me in these narratives.

HUO | Let's talk about *Cremaster*!

MB | I think that from the beginning, the *Cremaster* series was trying to take on a cinematic language that I had not dealt with before. I wanted to see how this sculptural project could align itself with the cinematic form, and still come out as a sculptural project. This was the first time that I had made a single-channel work, and it changed things knowing that they would be seen from the beginning to the end. When Jonathan and I started working together on *Cremaster 5*, a significant shift occurred. *Cremaster 5* was more linear, and more cinematic. Up to that point, I was still straddling two different types of structure. Somehow placing the musical narrative on top of the visual narrative after having developed the two simultaneously, gave this piece a different gravity. This really solidified the experiment.

HUO | How did the collaboration between the two of you start? How did you meet?

MB | We met through a mutual friend who was the director of photography of these projects. They had worked together previously. I was using found music for the *Cremaster 1* soundtrack, 1930s film music that belonged to the public domain. I needed to bridge between two pieces of found music, and Jonathan wrote some original material to create that connection. Shortly after that we started developing *Cremaster 5*, as an opera. I had no idea at the time what kind of demand that placed on a composer, but it seemed pretty straightforward at the time. [*laughs*]

HUO | Jonathan. How was the beginning of this collaboration from your perspective?

JB | It was interesting. When Matthew first came over, I did not know anything of his work. I had heard from Pete about a crazy guy who was working in the studio. He described some stuff to me. I think I felt he was quite different. I was coming from the idea of sound as the power of sound, it was all about performance and moments for me. Making a piece was about altering states and going into another world. At the time, I thought that this was not what I had been asked to do by Matthew, or what he was doing. Later on, after a while of feeling that he was quite different, I started to realize exactly what I needed to do. And that was a nice progression. The first project was more about musical facility, about taking an idea that Matthew had and then realizing it. It was interesting how little by little it became more of a collaboration, more of a shared responsibility.

HUO | Do you think that within the collaboration there is now a kind of situation that goes beyond the mere fact of being commissioned to do a soundtrack?

MB | I think because of the experience with *Cremaster 5*, because of its nature, the two things had to be developed simultaneously. We went to Budapest with the finished work of music, where Ursula Andress could lip-sync over the recording that we had already made. At the same time the music was being developed, the concept of the picture was being developed. That was very organic and very, very satisfying. I think what ended up happening was that, as we moved on to *Cremaster 2*, where there was not really a need to develop music before picture, we sort of did it anyway, or did it simultaneously in certain cases, because it was, for me, so helpful, just in developing the work in general, to have a sense of how it might sound.

HUO | You mentioned how the *Cremaster* grew out of the Kassel installation, a very architectural installation. I wanted to ask you about architecture and, specifically, about the Budapest experience in relation to architecture. Could you tell me about your interest in the opera space?

MB | I suppose it has to do with the stadium, and the relationship between the athlete and that architecture. In the way that Jim Otto is a psychological aspect of the field which the stadium holds—how quickly the stadium becomes a body. An image, which was useful for me, while making *Cremaster 1*, was the entrance into the stadium from the outside in, and from the inside out. Alternating views of passing up the ramps which wrap around the curved walls of the stadium, and passing through the long tunnels leading from the locker room to the field of play. In both cases, the sound of all of the people in the stadium is nearly overwhelming, though as the view reaches the place where the field can be seen, the stadium seats are empty, and there is nobody on the field. This started as some sort of waking dream, but I became preoccupied with this idea of how a work could have that quality, of activating a dormant body. Opera houses are even more like this in the way that they are built for acoustical reasons. They are built to mimic the resonant chamber inside the body. The opera house is a place where scale relationships are thrown off by the possibility that a small figure on stage is able to fill the architectural body with sound. I never understood why, in opera, they would turn the house lights down. I feel like the space is so much a part of the dynamic. Do you have any connection to the house?

JB | The issue of lights is something I've been thinking about. The idea of making a new opera was problematic in the sense that in a certain way the opera is a thing of the past. I think we are used to having the lights turned off. And that has something to do with the idea of the suspension of disbelief that happens when a performance starts. And I think to make a new opera you either have to turn the lights off and go for it that way, or you try to break everything. What is interesting about that is the fact that it is in that house. You turn the lights on. You go ahead and make an opera, but you also have the lights on, saying, "I am making an opera right now." So there is a certain self-consciousness to it, in the way the piece runs, where the Queen [in *Cremaster 5*] is singing about what is happening in the room in the opera house itself in the language of the opera. There is a story that is taking place, but we are also with her at the same time. I think that is one of the most fascinating things about it, especially in terms of making a new piece. It can be an opera and also be aware of itself. For me, there are a lot of layers.

HUO | *Cremaster* starts with the island in *Cremaster 4*, which is a confined zone. The opera, again, is a kind of confined zone. It has been said in relation to your work that you somehow infiltrate or infect such closed systems by bringing in some disturbance or shift or virus. *Cremaster 2* is more like a landscape.

MB | Yes. Although for my understanding of *Cremaster 2*, it is important for that landscape also functions as a sculptural body. It is possible to describe a sculptural form starting with the glacier fields in the Canadian Rockies, and passing down through the American Rockies, and on to the Bonneville Salt Flats in Utah. This cleft in the landscape was left behind by one massive glacier. This is the stadium or opera house which contains the *Cremaster 2* narrative, just as the island was to *Cremaster 4*, and the bridge and bathhouse were to *Cremaster 5*. We're currently working on *Cremaster 3* [2002] in the Chrysler building, and that works in a similar way. The concept was drawn, with five locations along a line on the map, from west to east. It seemed possible that these five sites could be singular sculptural entities, and one could draw a line between each of them—not just by me but by anybody.

HUO | And that master plan of these five spots was something you had mapped out from the beginning?

MB | Yes.

HUO | That leads me to the question of your method of working. Every time I visit your studio, I am not only very impressed by the incredible complexity of the sets that you built up in the studio, how the studio becomes denser and denser, but also by the storyboards which you display on the walls, which include drawings, postcards, photography, cut-outs of many things: a lot of research material. Could you tell me a little bit about your method of working, and the method of research in general, and about these storyboards?

MB | The storyboards started in a more traditional way as a drawing practice. I am thinking of storyboards that precede the *Cremaster* pieces. Those have very little other than drawing in them. The *Cremaster* storyboards brought in more and more layers of imagery from other sources. [*pause*] I am not really answering your question. I am not sure I can actually. I think it is an intuitive process that works for me, and I had never intended to exhibit them. It was simply a method. The exhibition that you made in Paris was the first time I exhibited them. It was interesting to see the storyboards trying to communicate in that way.

HUO | One of the things we have not yet spoken about is the question of casting, the question of you not only bringing in a composer and a range of different practitioners, but you also bring in actors, who are sometimes not actors. So I wanted to ask how Norman Mailer's *The Executioner's Song*[2] not only was an important point of departure for *Cremaster 2*, but also how you then brought in Norman Mailer as an actor?

MB | There is a constellation drawn in my understanding of Executioner's Song, between Mailer, Gary Gilmore and Harry Houdini. That made the choice to include Mailer in the piece seem very obvious. Mailer becomes paternal to Gilmore as the author of the book. Although it is mentioned only briefly in the book, Gilmore's grandmother allegedly had an affair with Harry Houdini at the World's Fair in 1893. This would make Gilmore Houdini's illegitimate grandson.

2 Norman Mailer, *The Executioner's Song* (New York: Little, Brown and Comp., 1979).

So the story became more to do with this leap from Gilmore's generation to Houdini's generation. It became a clear choice to cast Mailer as Houdini, as the paternal character in that constellation. Mailer looked an awful lot like Houdini when he was young, but the issue of likeness was not really the point at all in this. It had to do with that paternal constellation, and with the legacy of a kind of physicality that both Mailer and Houdini possessed. These characters are more like physical states rather than developed narrative characters. In the case of casting, somebody like Mailer brings with him the physicality in his writing style and his life to that role. These cultural figures that I gravitate toward tend to have a significant physicality. It has become an effective way keeping the character more in the physical sphere, rather than purely in the dramatic sphere.

HUO | That leads us to Richard Serra, whom you cast for your new piece.

MB | Yes, Richard is, of course, very good that way. And so is Ursula Andress in my opinion. There is a certain brutality to her, in the way that her athletic body redefined the feminine sex symbol. Her shoulders were bigger than her hips. She emerged from the sea carrying a knife. That had not been seen before.

JB | Is there a sense of their notoriety? They are seen by so many people, so does other people's image of them act as part of the material?

MB | I think it is completely different, depending on where it is seen and by whom. I am very interested in that possibility of multiple readings, and not just with those characters.

Obviously the Isle of Man TT Race is going to mean something completely different to somebody in Britain than to somebody in America who has never even heard of it. The same could be said true for the generational difference in the audience.

HUO | Serra might not be recognized outside the art world.

MB | Which also felt right to me. I suppose there was a logical step that the project could have taken towards cinematic form, and I felt pretty strongly against casting somebody who would advance the project in that way.

HUO | When I interviewed you a few years ago I asked you about your unrealized projects, and the big unrealized project you named was *Cremaster 3*, about the Chrysler building. Now you have realized your unrealized project. I wanted to ask about the location, about the building. Why did it have to be the Chrysler building?

MB | It is always hardest to talk about the thing that you are working on. There are a number of things about the Chrysler building that interest me. One, being that it is the corporate headquarters of a maker of vehicles. The building also has formal relationships to my language that are useful. Most important is that the building is a multi-faceted reflector. As it sits between the two halves of the story, it has the ability to reflect the various aspects of the project. As a mirror, it speaks to a level of narcissism or hubris that *Cremaster 3* possesses. For a moment, the entity of *Cremaster 3* believes that it can understand the entire form and see it from both directions simultaneously, when in fact it cannot.

HUO | Having spoken about *Cremaster 2* and *Cremaster 3*, it might be interesting to speak about how your collaboration evolved from one to the other.

MB | Yes, let's speak about where we are right now. Do you feel a big difference between what you are working on right now and the Utah project?

JB | For me, I think that I have more and more of an involvement in and an understanding of the whole thing. I felt that in *Cremaster 2*, the musical sections were entities within themselves. I always thought how that was in the whole picture, that each thing was kind of discrete in a way. I am finding that this one is more about figuring out the whole puzzle, in order to make one move and to then understand the other moves. This one feels like it is taking a lot longer because there are so many questions that need to fall in place. We have got much more of a language, much more of an understanding of each other, so that some things are more automatic. We don't really have to talk about stuff as much. That is good, and I am realizing it is also kind of difficult. I am not sure whether it is about responsibility.

HUO | How do you see it, Matthew?

MB | I could talk about some of the things that we are currently trying with the music in relationship to the site. I think it is interesting that the piece is set in 1929–30 when the Chrysler building was constructed. It has some relationship to the labor guilds . . . the stonemasons and the metalworkers. The story moves through the different floors of the building, moving toward the top of the building, where the spire functions as a transmitter, for radio and

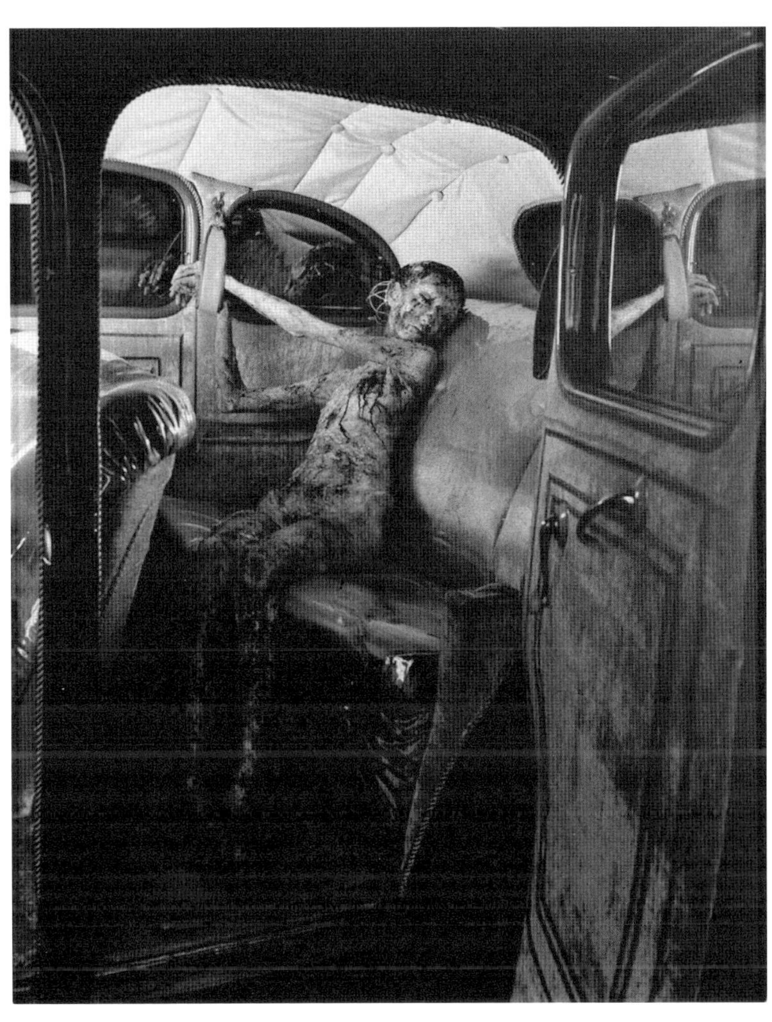

Cremaster 3, 2002
Production still

television companies. When the story arrives in that space in the spire, it loses its relationship to a specific period. It feels more like a video game. And many of the actors and characters that were in the film up to this point, appear in this game. The game takes place on the different levels of the Guggenheim Museum, and is theoretically transmitted back to the spire of the Chrysler building. There are five levels, which function as five different allegories of the five *Cremaster* chapters. And once the transmission is finished, the story ends with an epilogue in the Irish Sea, which is based on a very old creation myth of the Isle of Man, which is a battle between a giant in Scotland and a giant in Ireland. And this, we tried to shoot in a way that it really felt like a child's fairy tale. So you end up with a collision of urban 1930s music with a Celtic superimposition over that, with the combination of the digital space of the video game. It's an interesting juggling act for Jonathan.

HUO | So it is a traveling out, not only through space, but also through time.

MB | Yes, and musically it is maybe one of the more interesting problems we have had. With *Cremaster 2*, the Country and Western music's relationship to the American landscape and how that could become fused with Heavy Metal and other American genres like the Mormon choral singing, fell into place pretty easily, at least as an idea. This feels a lot more challenging, and might be taking us a little bit longer to sort out.

JB | There is also the idea of this prototypical kind of electronic music, of certain things that happened in the 1930s.

MB | Like the early synthesizers.

JB | Yes. And then dealing with that, and also digital space now.

HUO | You mentioned the Guggenheim. Besides the *Cremaster 3* projects you are working at the moment, you are also in the middle of preparing your biggest exhibition so far for the Guggenheim Museum, which is curated by Nancy Spector.[3]

MB | Yes, I was about to say that one of the other exciting things about this current work is that it is a return to thinking about architecture as a musical instrument. The escaping air from the elevator shafts . . . the reverb in the lobby . . . if the building could sing, what would it sound like? In these projects there is an approach with sound design that crosses over into the realm of music and that is exciting to me, especially when the music feels like it's growing out of the environment of the narrative. It gives the sound a site-specificity. This is also true of the approach I am taking with the Guggenheim exhibition, the way that it will be organized around the scenes from *Cremaster 3* that were made there. It will have a site-specificity similar to those exhibitions in '91 where there is a strong relationship between the action and the environment of the installation. That the Guggenheim has five levels ends up being a perfect organizing principle to make an encyclopedic show with the *Cremaster* cycle—beginning with *1* on the bottom and ending with *5* on the top.

HUO | Will there be anything outside the museum, on the façade?

3 *The Cremaster Cycle*, Guggenheim Musuem, New York; Museum Ludwig, Cologne; Musée d'art Moderne, Paris, 2002–03.

MB | Yes. The coat of arms of *Cremaster* will be on the façade. We're just starting to talk about the possibility of a parade at the beginning of the exhibition. I am thinking that it could function a little bit like the Palio, that it could start within the rotunda and then work its way out onto Fifth Avenue, and would focus primarily on the horses that appear in the scene in *Cremaster 3*. They are horses that are running but are dead. They are full body prosthetic suits that we made for ten racehorses. They have three layers of anatomy. There is a layer of bone, a layer of tendon and muscle, and a layer of skin, in various states of decay. The parade will be organized around the procession of horses.

HUO | Concerning the films. I saw in an exhibition at Portikus that you had actually developed a space for each film.[4] Will this be the case here also?

MB | It will be the case in certain venues. For instance, in Cologne there is a cinema space that has a very close proximity to the exhibition space itself, which makes it function very well within an museum environment, to have the moving image an integral part of the exhibition. Whereas in other locations, for instance in Paris, we will need to build a space to hold the moving image to try to make it central in the exhibition. In New York it will have the possibility of being a little more fractured. There is a cinema called Film Forum that has played all of the *Cremaster* pieces—it is downtown, and they will play the five films in a festival format. To play the new piece simultaneously, the museum has a theater space beneath the rotunda. It feels right to have the films considered in the same architectural footprint as

4 *Cremaster 5*, Portikus, Frankfurt am Main, 1997.

the exhibition, and try to put together special programs. I think every venue will have a different strategy on how to integrate the moving image. The real challenge of this exhibition is how to integrate the moving image with the sculpture.

HUO | Your works have been shown in cinemas, and there is also the idea of showing them on TV in the United States. You have explored lots of spaces outside the art space. Your work has gone far beyond the boundary of the art world in terms of its reception and its impact. So I was wondering what the function of the art world is for your work today, and, in general, how far you feel that the artwork needs to be protected?

MB | There are several questions in there. I think for me it is critical that all of these media come together as one form. The museum is the best place for that to happen. While it's true that the moving image can travel far beyond the walls of the museum—the further, the better—I think at the moment the museum is the place to make the overall form very clear.

HUO | Do you want to answer this question of the museum from your perspective as a composer?

JB | I guess I am interested in the idea that you cannot separate performance or music from its context. I am not very happy with most of the accepted contexts for music or ways of delivering music. People listen to it at home or in a concert hall. I think somehow the art context gives at least cause for thought about that, and also a kind of control. There is something about the awareness of the importance of the context that is really helpful for me. Also the idea that you are aware of your making. For me, this makes it go further out than it would if it was just out there somewhere.

HUO | Something we have not spoken about is the notion of the book, which has played an important role in your work from the very beginning. I was very stunned when I recently looked at all your catalogues. The very first catalogue you did for the San Francisco Museum of Modern Art in 1991 was a seemingly conventional catalogue, but was actually designed almost as an artist's book.[5] Ever since you have done all the *Cremaster* books as artist's books. Could you tell me about the importance of the medium of the book for your work, and if it is correct that the books may be seen as pieces?

MB | They are certainly pieces. I tend to think somewhat non-hierarchically about the work in the way that the different aspects are symbiotic. Over time you realize that the thing that most people see might not be what you expected in the beginning. It's the books that end up having the wider distribution, and that has influenced me. It interests me that the moving image is slowed down and crystallized in a particular way in the books, and that has a different kind of clarity than the films have. Some aspects of the films that are somewhat elusive become clearer in the books. For instance, the photography in the books, which is photographed rather than videotaped, tends to have a resolution and a kind of stillness that makes it possible to study the detail in a way that cannot happen in the moving image. I believe it ends up informing one's memory of the film. It was a surprise to

5 Matthew Barney and Robert R. Riley, *Matthew Barney: New Work* (San Francisco, CA: San Francisco Museum of Modern Art. 1991).

learn that it was working that way. The books function as manuals, and bring clues to the narrative.

HUO | Another question related to your books is that besides the editing and the sequencing and the layout that made them into artist's books, there is also a special feature. The *Cremaster* books have this plasticized cover with the stencil-like logo somehow printed into the plastic. I wondered if those are designed by you. They make the book into a sculpture.

MB | Yes, they are designed by me. I think book design started to excite me by the virtue that every spread has a gutter. And this started to align with some of the sculptural notions I was preoccupied with, to do with the natal cleft of the body, that line that has the memory of the initial cell division in our bodies, and how from that symmetry, an asymmetry can be introduced. And the book really lends itself to that, and the notion of the gatefold lends itself to that. In that way, the book can function as an orifice in certain ways—and with a slipcover or bellyband you can cancel or close the orifice. Considering book design began to feel like the relationship between the drawings and the framing of the drawings. There are various entrances and exits into the sculptural works. The books and the drawings function this way.

HUO | The project you mentioned last time has been realized, but I wanted to ask you what today, from all your unrealized projects, is a particularly important project.

MB | Within *Cremaster*, one unrealized project was the desire to make *Cremaster 4* a broadcast piece for television. While it was essentially an earthwork on the island, that would be abstracted as a secondary form, as a broadcast. If I am honest, that would have been the purest way to realize that work. I tried to do it, but could not make it happen. And this failure may have influenced the way the rest of the project was exhibited, in some way. The solution became the cinema, which became more and more appropriate in later chapters. I think *Cremaster 4* could have been really special as a broadcast around the time of the TT Race . . . as a form of infiltration.

HUO | What about your unbuilt roads?

JB | Most of what I am interested in now is happening or about to happen. I am interested in the idea of sound sources. The movie theater is a pretty interesting place to try to push that, within its standardized context. There are five speakers, so there is the ability to place sounds, which is not done very often. Usually, the rear speakers are just meant to give a feeling of some kind of presence with a sound effect. I am kind of looking forward to using that as part of the musical soundscape, and to use that to control the standardized environment to create certain physical effects. I had been interested in that before, but in a film theater context you could not count on the technology to provide that and to know how much power you would have.

MB | In our case you still can't count on it, at least in the context of the art-house cinema. I haven't talked about it much, the thing about being an art project and working at the scale of feature-length cinema . . . and coming up against the real financial constraints. In this case, the only places that would be interested in showing this work have financial and technological limitations.

JB | That is still true, but generally it is a bit better. We can at least commit a film to a format. I feel a little bit more confident about saying that a piece needs to be five channel and institutions coming up with it. Placement of sound in general, and I think also in the Guggenheim, the idea of having sound sources there, is interesting. For me, it's about relating back to the live thing.

HUO | So may I ask a question I forgot before? In the text by Richard Flood, he says that he had asked you on two occasions for a list of films. This includes Jean-Pierre Jeunet's *Delicatessen* [1991], *Female Trouble* [1974] by John Waters, Ken Russell, *Hellbound: Hellraiser II* [1988] by Tony Randall and *The Evil Dead* [1981]. He then mentions he attended this Richard Prince five-minute screening, where you chose five minutes out of *Society* [1989] by Brian Yuzna, an obscure film that I don't know. He said he asked you the question again, some years later, and you said, *Flying down to Rio* [1933], *Necromantik 2* [1991], *Olympia Part Two: Festival of Beauty* [1938], *The Shining* [1980], *Willy Wonka & the Chocolate Factory* [1971]. Is there anything to add to this list?

MB | I think my film consumption tends to be about what I am working on at the time. At that moment, the answers are pretty obvious. There is a German movie called *The Lift* [1983], about a possessed elevator [*laughs*], that does its passengers in: the doors open and a blind man walks in and falls to his death in the empty elevator shaft, things like that, one sight gag after another, but it is definitely in that genre of film that I love, where the evil is embodied in a piece of architecture. Then of course *The Fountainhead* [1949] and various other films from the 1930s that help with thinking about art direction in terms of what we're doing at the moment in the Chrysler building.

HUO | Alejandro Jodorowsky never popped up on the list? *El Topo* [1970]?

MB | I have seen *El Topo* and *The Holy Mountain* [1973], but . . .

JB | *The Bride with White Hair* [1993], *Swordsman II* [1992].

MB | Yes! The Hong Kong cinema films do have a kind of video game logic—we've been thinking about how our characters could move in that game space we're building.

HUO | To be continued. Thank you very much.

II Looking at *Drawing Restraint Vol. 1*[6]
phone call, February 2005

Hans Ulrich Obrist | The first image is a "cross-section of muscle and the muscle connective tissue harness. Individual muscle fibers are ganged into groups by connective tissue," so it's almost like a scientific presentation.

Matthew Barney | This is an attempt to try to establish a foundation for the *Drawing Restraint* concept. This selection of images is something along the lines of a storyboard for the larger *Drawing Restraint* narrative. The first pictures take the condition of hypertrophy, the way that muscles within the body develop, as an analogy for the creative process. I was thinking about the way muscle tissue within the body depends on resistance in order to grow and how this might make a case for resistance as a prerequisite for creativity.

6 Matthew Barney and Francis Mckee, *Drawing Restraint Vol. 1* (Cologne: Walther König, 2006).

The second image describes protein synthesis within the muscle tissue. It reads, "Each muscle fiber is composed of myofilaments, which are primarily made up of proteins. When the muscle is overloaded, protein synthesis increases, and the myofilaments thicken and increase in number." The third image shows how the connective tissue proliferates along with satellite cells that surround the muscle fibers. This process thickens and strengthens the muscle's connective tissue harness. This is hypertrophy. At a certain point, all of these biological facts started to feel useful as a way of describing a model for an aesthetic system.

HUO | You made a drawing called *Hypertrophy* [1991]. Does it basically describe this process?

MB | The principle of resistance training is that you exhaust your muscles, effectively tearing them down, then resting for a period to allow them to heal. During that healing period they become stronger and larger. I always imagined it as an ascending sine curve of growth and recovery. If you chart strength that way, your strength is increasing, but in order for it to increase it has to decrease as it's recovering. So again, I think there was, at a certain point, an attempt to take this biological fact, these ways of mapping the processes within the body, as a way of describing a larger aesthetic system.

HUO | What is also interesting is the question of time in art. Throughout the 1990s there was a very important discussion about time, time was reintroduced as a major factor and very early on you emphasized time. Your description of the process of hypertrophy can also be applied to the question of time.

MB | Certainly. In the course of this ascending sine curve, one has to accept that there will be plateaus of development, both in muscle mass, and in strength. You wait out these plateaus knowing that they are going to come eventually, and there are all sorts of philosophies about how to trick your body out of a plateau of suspended development. Certain training programs believe that if you take your body into a state of total exhaustion, where you really can't physically go any further, and you proceed to train by lifting the resistance with the assistance of another persons strength, that you can fool your muscle cells. Somehow the cells will continue to reproduce during these assisted "forced repetitions" in spite of the fact that you are really only providing 5% to 10% of the strength. I guess ideas like this, where an odd intersection exists between a biological and a psychological condition, were central to the first narrative pieces I made.

HUO | The cover of the book features a drawing with three elements, which you refer to as "three phases of a system: Situation, Condition and Production." Maybe it would be interesting if you gave a brief definition of those three elements and the way they interact.

MB | These three terms are used to describe a three-phase cycle called "The Path." The Path is a meditation on the creative process. Situation would be characterized as raw drive or hunger. It's where subject matter is indiscriminately consumed, driven by undifferentiated sexual energy. In this phase, the energy in the system was visualized as undirected and unable to generate form. Condition becomes a visualization of a disciplinary funnel that could take the raw, useless energy in Situation and channel it into something useful. Condition takes content that Situation had consumed and begins to give it form. In the Production phase, a form begins to emerge. If The Path could be visualized as a digestive tract, Production is it's anal or oral output. Eventually, the goal of The Path was to abstract the form of Production, and to create a loop between Situation and Production. The form was called Bolus, and took the shape of a small hand weight. I imagined it as an ingested wad of matter, offering nutrients as it moved through the system, transforming as it passed through the disciplinary funnel. The Bolus also functioned as an external connection between Situation and Condition. In that sense, the *Drawing Restraint* project is a kind of cross fertilization between the desire to make, and the discipline to continue making, while trying not to let creative energy dissipate by allowing one's practice to take a concrete form.

HUO | And that changes because you actually end on that page with the sentence: "This form enables a meditation and endless loop between desire and discipline." The appendix is usually the end of the book. At the same time you are talking here of an infinite process, which doesn't end.

MB | I guess that all of that language depends on accepting the body as perforated. The body has primary entry points and primary exit points, but there are also a number of secondary valves; it's full of holes. This is the model that led to the stories in the narrative projects that came after the early *Drawing Restraint* pieces; they were a manifestation of that idea of a body that was full of holes. In those stories there was an interest in expressing the conflict between inhabiting a very hermetic, internal place, where everything made sense, and the desire to communicate as an artist. I think that is what the conflict in The Path is about and that is what the narrative in the Otto and Houdini stories were about. Some of the *Cremaster* narratives address that as well.

HUO | Throughout this appendix there are questions related to the previous point of production. I was wondering to what extent *Drawing Restraint* has to do with injecting a doubt into production.

MB | There was a kind of play on words that I was interested in when I was making these first pieces, which had to do with the word "facility." If this aesthetic system were effective as a system, then the system needed a facility. I think I wanted to visualize it in institutional terms somehow. As I started building these rooms where the experiments were to take place, I was thinking about them and calling them facilities. At the same time the word "facility," or "facile," seemed appropriate to what it felt like to sit down and make a drawing without some kind of external resistance, or without a program. In that sense I think there was a feeling of doubt about the endeavor, sitting down and making a drawing, saying, "I am done with this drawing; this is a finished drawing." The *Drawing Restraint* endeavor had something to do with undermining that in a certain way.

HUO | We have had a lot of discussions before about the relation between *Drawing Restraint* and the *Cremaster* cycle in which you've said that *Drawing Restraint* anticipated the *Cremaster* cycle. You also said that there are a lot of similarities. One of the basic differences, I think, is related somehow to production. With *Cremaster*, even if you self-produced large parts of it, there was still a dependence on other people, on camera people and actors, whilst the *Drawing Restraint* is about studio experiments or it is situations where you actually don't depend on anybody to do it or re-do it. Can you say something about the similarities and the differences between *Drawing Restraint* and the *Cremaster* cycle?

MB | I guess *Drawing Restraint 7* was both a precursor to the *Cremaster* cycle and some sort of transitional piece within the *Drawing Restraint* language. It provided a narrative transition to *Drawing Restraint 9* [2005], which I'm working on now. Both pieces described resistance as a psychological condition, or as conflict within a larger narrative, rather than describing a literal, physical condition of restraint. *Drawing Restraint 9* is very much dependent on the structure that you are talking about, a collaborative structure, a team structure. Ultimately, I feel like the idea of the *Drawing Restraint* can operate in both ways: both as solitary studio experiments, as well as in a more narrative, cinematic way.

HUO | It's also a question of the tools. The tools in use change throughout the *Drawing Restraint* project.

MB | They do. The majority of them, of course, were made between 1987 and 1989 so I would say that those tools were all quite similar. They were all taken more or less directly from athletic training and from this meditation on hypertrophy and other biological models. *Drawing Restraint 7* came five years later. At the time I had just finished the Otto/Houdini pieces and had become quite addicted to storytelling. I had started developing characters that came from my experiences as an athlete and integrated them with characters that were coming from my relationship to film and to other forms of storytelling. *Drawing Restraint 7*, I guess, was an attempt to prove to myself that the *Drawing Restraint* project could still function with a new set of tools.

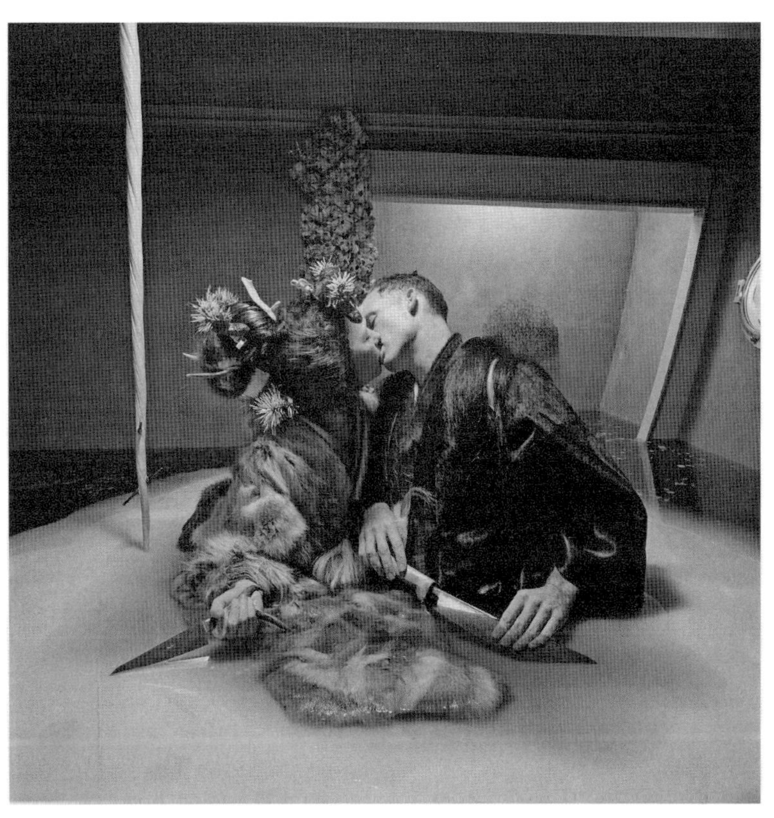

Drawing Restraint 9: Shimenawa, 2005
C-print in self-lubricating plastic frame
43 x 43 x 1 1/2 inches

HUO | One of the *Drawing Restraints* was re-done because there were no documents. There is also a little bit of this idea that the reader could do it.

MB | The spirit of some of those first *Drawing Restraint* pieces was really about creating a facility that anybody could enter. I think that they were built more for my own needs, but I also invited friends to come in and use them. In that sense re-performing a *Drawing Restraint* doesn't feel awkward to me.

HUO | While working on this book we discussed the notion of it being, particularly for *1–7*, an archive in black and white and suddenly we jump into the present tense in some way with color. This is something I have never experienced with a book before: we have the archive and we have the present.

MB | The leaps that take place between *Drawing Restraint 2* [1988] and *3* [1988], and between *6* [1989] and *7* are significant in the way that the real time experiment becomes more and more narrative, but those leaps are expressed in a rather subtle way in the book. I wanted to make the difference between *7* and *8* more extreme. *Drawing Restraint 8* [2003] is about removing the restraint from the system as a way to activate an erotic gesture. *Drawing Restraint* didn't allow for eroticism, in much the same way that it couldn't allow the production phase to express itself. In *Drawing Restraint 8*, the body was visualized as liberated from its restraint, and libidinous. It was also beginning to atrophy. This is the narrative condition for *Drawing Restraint 9*.

III Discussing *Drawing Restraint Vol. 5*,[7] 2006

Hans Ulrich Obrist | I read a book the other day that could be useful.

Matthew Barney | You should suggest some stuff.

HUO | Don DeLillo would be interesting. Well, there is *Cosmopolis*,[8] which you read; that is his most recent book. There is also *The Body Artist*.[9] There is obviously *Mao II*.[10] I don't know if you have material or a text related to *Drawing Restraint* that we could send to him.

MB | It would be very easy to write a couple of paragraphs. It would be something along the lines of describing a series

7 Matthew Barney and Neville Wakefield, *Drawing Restraint Vol. 5* (Cologne: Walther König, 2008).
8 Don DeLillo, *Cosmopolis* (New York: Scribner, 2003).
9 Don DeLillo, *The Body Artist* (New York: Scribner, 2001).
10 Don DeLillo, *Mao II* (New York: Scribner, 1991).

of studio experiments that had to do with building a facility that would overcome the facility of drawing. And that it started as a meditation of the physical dynamic of muscle development of the body as a metaphor for the development of form.

HUO | How did the title come about, because that was there from the very beginning, wasn't it?

MB | I guess "restraint" was. When you are talking about muscle development the word that is usually used is "resistance," as in "resistance training": resistance against what the mechanical apparatus will give you. But with "restraint" I was interested in making it more a psychological proposal about trying to sublimate a negativity somehow; to sublimate a bondage of some sort. It was a long time ago! [*laughs*]

HUO | It comes before *Cremaster* and after *Cremaster*, so it is almost like the whole thing around it.

MB | That was right before I made *REPRESSIA* [1991]. It was the same thing. I think that at that time I was particularly interested in taking words that were associated with restrictive, psychological situations and trying to create a positive language.

HUO | In the 1960s a lot of artists worked between drawing and performance.

MB | Yeah, for sure. There were things like Gordon Matta-Clark, his cutting pieces. I don't think I knew so much about those things that Carolee Schneemann did. I knew about those later.

HUO | I'm wondering what might be the common thread running through *Drawing Restraint*, about what binds it, and it might be in the idea of there not being a public?

MB | Right. It is a meditation on studio practice. Or on athletic training. The *Drawing Restraint* pieces were done at a time when I was trying to figure out how that psychological space of training, and that dialogue you have with your body, could become there. *Field Dressing* [1989] was one of them that started to try to do that. It led to those pieces that I showed with Barbara [Gladstone Gallery, New York] and Stuart [Regen Gallery, Los Angeles], those pieces with Jim Otto and Harry Houdini. That definitely grew out of *Drawing Restraint*: the idea that the internal dialogue of that you have with your body could become narrative.

HUO | You mentioned that this happens in sequence. Would you say that *1* to *4* is a sort of prelude without narration?

MB | Well, actually, no. I think there is a progression.

HUO | So in each one there is more?

MB | Yeah, and I think that that is how the book could function. I think this break between black and white and color could really emphasize that.

HUO | *Drawing Restraint 1* to *7* is an archive, in black and white, and then there is the color for the present.

MB | Conceivably you could even do some kind of a transitional thing with histories. To do that it would require some kind of a fade in. You know, like, dialing a color in rather than it being a break. You would use this piece as a way of feathering the color in. The Wizard of Oz piece is really appealing. I also think it would be really interesting for the fiction to respond to that somehow.

HUO | Well, that's another interesting thought: last time you were speaking about the art form and you said that an artist's book shouldn't have a secondary text, say, by a curator or an art critic, since that's like implying there is another artist. And so you suggested Don DeLillo. So that is something that we should mention in a few words: why him?

MB | I read *End Zone*,[11] this book about football that he wrote, when I was younger. I believe that I've read essays and shorter things by him and, in certain cases, things that had a stylistic similarity to Ballard with a kind of technocratic language that I respond to. I think that this book could function that way, with these descriptions of approaching synthesis and what is actually happening within the body: the body's own resistance.

HUO | So a kind of scientific language.

MB | Right, and these captions are written that way. I think another thing that would be important is to find some way of making it open-ended: implying that this project isn't finished.

11 Don DeLillo, *End Zone* (Boston: Houghton Mifflin, 1972).

HUO | Nine is the last one or will there be a following one afterwards?

MB | I have no idea, but I would say that it would be more interesting for the book to imply that it could continue.

HUO | Another dimension that is really interesting is that the San Francisco catalogue was really a catalogue, but from then on, really early in the 1990s, you suddenly no longer developed catalogues but instead artist's books. I wonder if from the beginning there was a sort of consciousness that this is what you wanted to do: artist's manuals?

MB | I think the manual thing was always part of the program: that it wasn't a catalogue or any kind of explication that was necessary, but rather it was about organizing the ideas into a manual, and that they weren't exhibitions that were being made but rather facilities. And a facility needs a binder, a manual. I actually think that I found a lot about that with that San Francisco book, in spite of the fact that it probably feels a bit more like a catalogue. I think I had certain restrictions with that book, with how the essay would function, and the works in the collection and the works in the exhibition would need to appear somewhere, but there is a whole index in that book.

HUO | So the form is announced there.

MB | Yeah. It is something to do with programs too, like programs when you go to a sports event and the program you are given describes the characters on the field, gives some autobiographical information about then. I think that when I started making this book I was thinking about how they could operate somewhat like a program: that they would give you highlights of the action, but they would also describe—as in portraiture—the characters and lay out the team. You know, this team versus that team.

HUO | So the cast. That is obviously different with *Drawing Restraint*, because as opposed to the *Cremaster* team, with such a dense form of collaboration, in *Drawing Restraint*, it is all you.

MB | Right. So this book shouldn't lose that quality of these pieces. This one in particular, but also the earlier ones that were really experimental. Really, the only thing left is ephemeral.

HUO | So, no object?

MB | It wasn't to do with production so much.

HUO | Maybe the last thing that we haven't spoken about is the scientific implications. I'm not sure I've understood completely the scientific source. Does it come from medical books or is it something else?

MB | Physiology books. Certainly those images in the lecture came from physiology books and some of those descriptions I copied out of physiology books and others I wrote myself. So I guess that is something we need to consider: how that can be rewritten and credited.

IV Bull, 2007
with Jonathan Bepler

[*watching a video of a bull in a field*]

Hans Ulrich Obrist | Now it is clear that his legs are quite rigid. It's interesting. He kind of drags them behind. So how old is he?

Mathew Barney | I don't know precisely, but I bet he's in the neighborhood of twenty years old. He's well passed his prime. If he doesn't work we need to find another older bull, but maybe not quite as old.

HUO | And what are the other animals? They are pigs?

MB | Yes. They're not as interesting. Wild boar are pretty interesting.

HUO | They can run very fast.

MB | Yes. We need to hit the road pretty soon, right, to get to the airport.

HUO | As Kurt Cobain would say, "You can't complain, you're on a plane."

MB | *[laughs]*

[in the car]

HUO | Let's start with a pre-coffee interview. We have just been visiting bulls, so maybe it would be nice to talk about the Manchester piece.[12] Last time we met, in Iceland last summer, the piece was still in a very different place. How has it evolved since then?

MB | When we talked then there was this ambition to take the Norman Mailer text and make a piece based on the first one hundred pages of *Ancient Evenings*.[13] As Jonathan and I started talking about that and developing that, it very quickly became much too long and complicated to do in this group show format. So we cut it into pieces and looked at the different scenes and tried to come up with one that would be a contender and one that could live on its own. We decided to develop the scene involving a bull. So that's what we're doing. It's still very related to the original idea but it's a little less ambitious.

HUO | You also mentioned a link to *Cremaster*.

12 *Guardian of the Veil* [2007] for *Il Tempo del Postino* at the Manchester International Festival, 2007.
13 Norman Mailer, *Ancient Evenings* (New York: Little, Brown and Comp., 1983).

MB | Yes, which is something that would make this different from what could eventually be this longer, evening-length piece. We thought it would be interesting to take the demolition car from *Cremaster 3* and use that as the vehicle that the bull interacts with. So in a certain way it is a collision of these two languages, the Celtic language of *Cremaster 3* and the Egyptian language of *Ancient Evenings*. As the *Ancient Evenings* language is to do with funerary practice in Egypt, this becomes something like a funeral for *Cremaster*.

HUO | Nancy Spector wrote that *Drawing Restraint* was important to *Cremaster* and now one can say it's almost the opposite with *Cremaster* being the portal: it goes back, or goes forward.

MB | Yes. It's nice to have this car out again, to look at it. It's been in storage since we shot that sequence in 2001. So often these objects are abstracted into sculpture and other things are either buried in deep storage, put in the prop category, and not really developed. I never really did anything with the car. I made a sculpture based on the cars, but the cars themselves were either destroyed or, in the case of this one, saved, but I haven't really looked at it since. It has pretty interesting energy about it.

HUO | So it's a prop with a potential in some way.

MB | Yes. It's the first time I've done this, to resurrect something like that, exhume it and try to take it somewhere else.

HUO | The opera in Vienna is the next chapter, one could say, in your very long on-going collaboration. You said the Manchester piece may link to a full-evening piece.

MB | Yes, definitely. It gives us a chance to begin to develop something like a template or a beginning of a map to expand into this other idea. For Jonathan it's probably a little less so, because it's more within his range already. I've just never really done a work on stage, so there is something quite terrifying about it for me.

HUO | So it's the very first time?

MB | Yes. I've certainly done performance but I think that putting something on stage is very different from that. It helps to start in a smaller way.

Jonathan Bepler | It feels a little bit freed from the idea of performance or of doing a show because it's bringing in the funerary idea. It's like bringing a ritual into that space. It makes me think of the idea that the opera house is one of the few places that has a musical entity built into it, almost as part of the architecture; there's always an orchestra there. So it can be less of a performance and more of a ritual there, letting the architecture and the music be part of that, letting the orchestra be part of the architecture and seeing how that breathes or what kind of life it has. It's not so much about showing something like in a performance, but somehow trying to activate the space, which feels what is happening with this ritual that's being performed. Less of a show, more something that is really being delivered. [*laughs*]

HUO | So how can one imagine that full evening? Do you already have a script for that opera? Will it be a sort of passe-partout, so that if you see the beginning you can maybe imagine the whole?

MB | Yes, there's a synopsis that certainly needs a lot of work at this point, but we are already up to about seven scenes. I would say the structure is in place and of course, working with Mailer's book, a lot of the text is in place, which is nice. It's a delight to be working with his words again.

HUO | It's like a gift that he came to you with this book; it's very unexpected. It's not that you appropriated it: he brought it to you.

MB | Yes.

JB | Doing the one scene as part of the bigger piece we are reminded that seeing one fragment of a larger work could be a whole story in itself and I think the depth of understanding it gives you from doing it that way—taking a fragment and doing it as an entire piece—is really strong. In the same way, Matthew got the book quite a long time ago and so some years later there are layers of experience behind him that inform it.

HUO | I have never really experienced being so close to a bull before today. That's a feature of these collaborations; whenever we work on a project it leads to totally new experiences.

MB | Yes. Well, in the Egyptian system the bull is one of the main animal deities. The Apis bull is connected to Osiris, so it's the most important of these animal manifestations. Given the nature of Mailer's text, what seems to be at the core of his story is that the gods are obliged to transform constantly and they are obliged to move between an animal state and a human state and to fuck one another and to kill one another and just to keep changing that way, folding themselves into each other. I wanted to develop a scene that could address that somehow, so in this scene the bull is mounting the back of this automobile and fucking this automobile. In the sense that this scene is a collision between the *Cremaster* language and the *Ancient Evenings* language, I would say it's both some sort of funeral rite for the *Cremaster 3* demolition car and a fertility rite, the possibility of resurrecting something and reactivating it. We still have a couple of contenders for the bull. Lord Rannoch may or may not be the final bull cast, but we are considering these highland bulls because they're indigenous to this part of the world, both in the sense that this performance is taking place in Manchester but also because the *Cremaster 3* language is Celtic. We are also considering some black bulls, which would be more consistent with the Egyptian narrative; the Apis bull was always black and had white in its tail that would separate into two strands and it had a white diamond on its forehead. The Apis bull actually had a beetle silhouette under its toe. These were the criteria for finding an Apis bull. When they died they were mummified. The most significant funeral of any living creature, human or otherwise, would be given to the Apis bull. They would then have to find another one, so a contingency of priests would travel all over the place looking for a bull that had these markings.

HUO | So does this very strong presence of the bull also have an impact on the sonic dimension?

JB | Yes, trying to react to it, not necessarily subjectively, but staying away from this obvious bull call.

MB | That would be the most obvious way of responding to the bull.

JB | I think it would be the big brass instruments, wouldn't it. The big, low, sound. I was thinking of the idea of capturing the insides of the bull, the inner intestines and maybe testicles, using low brass but in this more relaxed kind of bubbling way. But it's difficult.

HUO | So on the stage, in terms of the visual presence and the sonic presence, is there a contrast?

MB | Well there's going to be a contrast between part of the action entering from the back stage and part of the action entering through the house and I think the way we are talking about it now, both of these groups would have a musical dimension as well. So you'll have that kind of conflict happening, which could be very exciting, in the way that Jonathan's talking about the architecture having a sectioned musical component to it. That includes both backstage and auditorium as well. Otherwise, if I understand your question, in the way that the narratives I've done in the past tend to be very much about setting up a conflict, I would say this isn't so much about that. It's a procession. In that way all the characters are in a consensus in terms of what they're doing.

HUO | So there's a difference to previous narratives?

MB | You could say that, yes. There is certainly conflict in the larger *Ancient Evenings* narrative.

HUO | How would you answer that same question for the sound?

JB | I'm not sure why I'm thinking of the musical elements as being a little antagonistic. Maybe it has to do with describing different aspects of the same thing at the same time. If there's one group that's placed in the very upper part of the theater, another group that's placed in the rear of the stage, for example, they are pretty far from each other, so I have the feeling that they're calling to each other, but at the same time almost yelling at each other. So maybe it's just that inherent conflict in high and low and far and near and the idea of what the function of music is for the ritual or for the procession. There's a kind of calling, an inviting; at the same time there's a demanding, an insistence.

MB | I think that can be said of the intervention in general with the house, right? I don't know if we'll be able to get the permits to do this but we want to start the procession of the bull by bringing him from the street and into the lobby of the house and have a kind of coronation of this bull right in the lobby in the middle of the intermission. He would be pushed into the lobby surrounded by a rope to protect people but it would be a very aggressive act to bring him into the audience during the intermission and basically interrupt their intermission.

HUO | Creating, maybe, panic on the streets of Manchester?

MB | Perhaps. There is a way that the piece has that kind of conflict in it, even with what's taking place on stage, but I think compared to other things that we've done, the narrative is less to do with a conflict.

HUO | This is all happening a few months before your next very strong presence in the UK, which will be focused on *Drawing Restraint 9* at the Serpentine Gallery. So if the Manchester piece is the funeral of *Cremaster*, what is the link to *Drawing Restraint*?

MB | *Drawing Restraint* spans lot of creative time, so in that way it's been a lot of different things to me at different points in time. But most recently with *Drawing Restraint 9, 10, 11, 12, 13, 14, 15*, the works that have been done in the last two years, probably most significantly *Drawing Restraint 9*, which was filmed on a whaling ship, I was really craving a working condition that would put me in closer contact to the world or to a real environment, rather than the more controlled hermetic environment of *Cremaster*. To go and make a piece on a whaling ship and use the crew as the cast and to make this sculpture in real time on that ship was all really important for me. I would say it could be looked at as a bridge to this idea of making a piece on stage or to making live performance, making something that's even more actual than drawing a straight line or something that takes place in real time and takes place in front of a live audience, or potentially could take place in front of no audience, but does take place in actual time and space; it's not edited.

HUO | That's interesting. You told me last year it had to do with how you see the world, that you felt there was a desire to maybe get away from edited time and have the whole notion of performance become important again.

MB | Yes, it was a speculation. That obviously has to do with my own desire but, yes, I think that might be true. I don't know. Does that make any sense to you, Jonathan? Are you getting tired of receiving, of having to dig through layers and layers of media find, of mediated material, to get to the core of something? You're vested in performance in a way and you always have been, so it's probably different for you.

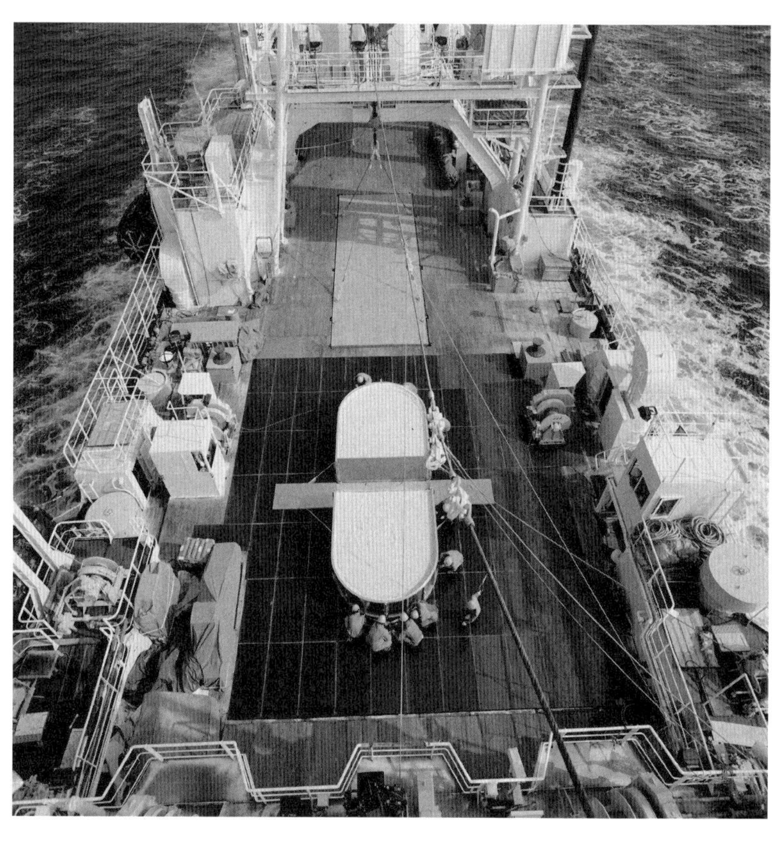

Drawing Restraint 9, 2005
Production still

JB | Yes but I've been doing a lot of film stuff and there's something about the length of time you have between performing something and using it, somehow, and having all this time to edit, which I find pretty uncomfortable.

HUO | So you agree?

JB | Yes. There's something really refreshing about the idea that something happens and is immediately released. For example, with the idea of spreading the orchestra around so there's no real focal point for the sound and the sound experience would then be quite different from one person to the next. With a live thing, if someone blinks or if someone coughs, then they miss some really important moments but there is something refreshing about that, I think.

MB | Coffee?

HUO | Fantastic: a coffee break.

[*in car, post-coffee*]

HUO | While we had a coffee a new idea popped up for the bull.

MB | Yes. Given the bull's age and his arthritic condition, we'll rig some sort of apparatus that would lift the front of Lord Rannoch onto the cow dummy. That rig would be within the language of geriatric aid apparatus, whatever that means. That stuff always looks the same.

JB | Blue-grey rubber.

MB | Yes, blue-grey rubber and aluminum. It could look like an enlarged walker that would be slid underneath him. [*laughs*]

HUO | So that makes it less rodeo and more opera?

MB | Yes. Exactly.

HUO | When I saw Lord Rannoch today he didn't remind me so much of rodeo.

MB | No. It's more like... do you remember the story of Ferdinand the Bull who slept all day under the cork tree? I don't remember how it ends, I just remember that he slept forever.

HUO | Surrounded by chicken and flies.

MB | Yes.

HUO | Another thing which has happened since we recorded last summer is there have been new chapters in the *Drawing Restraint* project. We discussed *Drawing Restraint 9* and now it has evolved quite a lot. We are now at number *15*. What has happened since *9*?

MB | Since *9*, numbers *10* and *11* were done in Kanazawa when there was an opportunity to make a survey exhibition of the *Drawing Restraint* work in Japan.[14] I thought it was important to make a couple of site-specific pieces that would relate more to the first *Drawing Restraint* pieces, a more direct approach after having taken a more cinematic

14 *Drawing Restraint*, 21st Century Museum of Contemporary Art, Kanazawa, 2005.

approach with number *9*. So *10* was like *6*; it was a trampoline that was used to make a drawing on a ceiling within the museum. *11* came about because I got interested in the idea of climbing through the exhibition and making a drawing above it. What happened was, a portrait room was hung with all the photography from *9* and then a climbing path was made through each of the walls of the portrait gallery and a drawing was made at the top of each of those walls. Number *12* [2005] was very similar to *10*, but this was done in the Leeum Samsung Museum in Seoul.

HUO | In the Rem Koolhaas building.

MB | That's right.

HUO | And you mentioned last time when we spoke that it was an interesting experience, this building, which is a sort of a black box.

MB | One of the features of that architecture became the focus of *12*. It was the place where this interior black box kissed up against the exterior walls. It was something like a natural feature in a climbing face that would really define the nature of that climb. Often a crack would be that way or an overhang or some sort of feature like that. So where those two volumes nearly touched, a climb passed through that. *13* [2006] was exciting for me; it was maybe somewhere in-between these two sensibilities. It was narrative in one way, where the General MacArthur character was shown leaving this abstraction of a landing craft. He walked through the petroleum jelly casting and walked across the gallery floor and arrived at a table that was made in the proportion of the table used to sign the Japanese Instrument of Surrender. All the drawings from the exhibition were signed on that table, both by myself, in the costume of General MacArthur, and by a Japanese delegate. So it also functioned as a way of completing that exhibition in the way that it had both a narrative program and a somewhat functional program. I enjoyed the duality that that piece had. Functional in the sense that it wasn't even exhibited in that exhibition:[15] the video document or the photographic documents weren't exhibited, it was just the object and the drawings that were signed and the actions.

HUO | In the book here you glued in a letter. Can you talk about this letter?

MB | Yes. When I was developing the *Drawing Restraint 9* story there was a moment when I thought General MacArthur needed to be present in that story as a character and in the first scripts there was a scene at the very beginning of the film where MacArthur would be sitting, smoking his pipe in one of his big clawed armchairs and effectively smoking the last breath from his corn cob pipe and a mushroom cloud would emerge from the pipe and the entire *Drawing Restraint 9* story would come out of that mushroom cloud. It started to feel like it would derail the rest of the story for it to start off so heavy-handedly, so eventually I came to the idea that this letter would be sung at the beginning of the film and would be a letter that would be written to General MacArthur from a Japanese citizen. I found a compilation of letters written to MacArthur and took one of them and manipulated it slightly and that's the song that Will Oldham sings at the beginning of *Drawing Restraint 9*.

15 *Occidental Guest*, Gladstone Gallery, New York, 2006.

HUO | And then it moves down to San Francisco, where I saw the exhibition.[16]

MB | That's right. Number *14* [2006] was somewhat of a horizontal version of numbers *11* and *12*. I climbed through the survey exhibition.

HUO | You basically climbed into that atrium.

MB | That's right. That was the first time in a while where I truly exhausted myself doing one of these pieces.

HUO | So it was very much about endurance.

MB | Yes. It was maybe also something to do with aging! [*laughs*] I couldn't control the line that I was drawing anymore and that was kind of interesting because I think at one point that was what it was about for me: really being exhausted and taking away the facile mark-making ability. It hasn't been that way for a long time. *15* [2007] took place on a transatlantic boat crossing.

HUO | That is the one I have not seen, which will also be part of the Serpentine show,[17] which is part of a new series of drawings you made on your boat.

MB | That's right. So there were a number of these trials that were set up on the boat.

HUO | Trials?

16 *Drawing Restraint*, San Francisco Museum of Modern Art, San Francisco, 2006.
17 *Drawing Restraint*, Serpentine Gallery, London, 2007.

MB | Yes, different drawing situations. I made a drawing in the chain locker, which was a very confined space, down under where you can't see out. A lot of it had to do with the fact that I get quite seasick on boats and was imagining that making drawings in these more confined places would really make me ill. In a funny way it didn't and I didn't really end up getting sick beyond the first couple of days.

HUO | That means it's more than an endurance piece, it's a really long piece because it took weeks to make.

MB | Right. I tried to set up a different situation every day.

HUO | So it was a daily practice of drawing?

MB | Yes. There were situations like making a drawing in the machine room, the engine room, making a drawing suspending myself off the edge of the foredeck and making a drawing in the hold. I made a drawing using a fish that we caught. Some of them are quite absurd and some of them are more endurance-related and some of them are made in bed and they are more controlled. It's a pretty wide range.

HUO | The result is basically a series of drawings.

MB | That's right.

JB | Did you have any vomiting?

MB | Yes, there was some vomiting.

JB | You were hanging off the side when the boat was running on the winch thing?

MB | Yes. It's hilarious.

HUO | On the boat it became, by definition, a daily practice of drawing, but I have the feeling, also through the focus of the *Drawing Restraint* series, there is a much bigger presence of drawings in your exhibitions. Could you maybe talk about that daily practice of drawing?

MB | I draw drawings like this, looking at this book.[18] I can't draw like that very often, so in that way I wouldn't call that a daily practice at all. In fact it's pretty rare where I'm in a place where I can sit down and make a drawing like that. I think it's one of the reasons why I find it so exciting, because I don't have access to it very often. But I draw a lot as a way of sketching out ideas or things that are being fabricated or even trying to make maps, like mapping out these ideas that are being worked on by a number of people in the studio. So drawing functions in a number of different ways for me. So in the broader sense it's a daily practice but in the more refined sense it's not at all as much as I wish it was.

HUO | I had the feeling when we talked about your drawings in the context of, for example, the *Voila* exhibition[19] it had a lot to do with storyboards and drawings you made in preparation for exhibitions of films and it was all about process.

MB | I think that drawings like this come last. In fact, a number of the drawings in this group are either aspects of the narrative that didn't come to the surface in the making of the film or even in the making of the sculpture, they came

18 Matthew Barney, Itsuko Hasegawa and Shin'Ichi Nakazawa, *Matthew Barney: Drawing Restraint Vol. 2* (Tokyo: Uplink, 2006).
19 *Voila: Le Monde dans la tête*, Musée d'Art Moderne, Paris, 2000.

after the film. These are buried notions that are within the same universe or, more, they are elaborations on a character or a sculpture that distils that character or form further. So in that sense drawings like this are the last stop or stage of making one of these larger narrative works that include film and sculpture and drawing.

HUO | So they are the first stage and then the last stage; pre-drawings and post-drawings.

MB | That's right, yes.

HUO | And the pre-drawings are more about sketching the ideas. What then is the role of the post-drawings? Are they made for exhibitions or are they also partially unrealized aspects, maybe, of the narrative?

MB | I think they are something like making *Drawing Restraint 10* after making number *9*. There is probably a need for me to be able to both spend two or three years making one thing and then to be able to turn around and make something in two hours. I think I have a need to be able to reclaim the ability to make it myself and put it all into one frame like that and I think the drawing is the only way I have been able to figure out how to do that.

HUO | Thinking about this evolution from *14* to *15* brings us to the boat trip and then to London and the Serpentine show. Will there be any other *Drawing Restraints* beforehand or how will it evolve?

MB | I think not. All my energy and all the studio's energy is devoted right now to testing and fabricating parts for the Manchester piece, so I don't think there's going to be any time to do that. Once July comes around we'll be giving up to come to Manchester.

HUO | The project which the two of you are doing in Manchester is the funeral of *Cremaster*, but there doesn't seem to be an end in sight for *Drawing Restraint*. It seems like a permanent project that will go on.

MB | Yes, definitely. I think that it functions something like a reset switch that brings me back to a starting place where the drawing can function in the way that it does as a source.

HUO | A question I have asked you many times before but each time the context changes so that's why I ask it again, is the question of your unrealized projects. Are there any projects of the scale of *Cremaster* that are so far unrealized? Any utopian projects?

MB | No. I think there are only a couple of false starts. Even something like *Cremaster* was still done in a pretty organic way; there was a kind of map that was made of the five locations and a very general notion of how those different locations would generate these individual narratives and then they were written and executed one at a time. It would be hard to imagine there being an unrealized evolved thing because I don't work that way. I think it's actually important for me that I understand that it's going to be shown and it's going to function as a communicative device in a certain way. I think it is important for me that there is an exhibition channel connected to it before it gets too evolved.

HUO | So in this sense one can say the unrealized project is the project which starts in Manchester and will then develop into a full-evening piece.

MB | Yes. Yet unrealized.

HUO | Do you know yet where it might be realized after Manchester?

MB | No, I don't.

HUO | So it could be any major opera house?

MB | At this point I'm not completely convinced it needs to happen on a proscenium stage, actually. Jonathan and I both have somewhat of an interest for that to happen but we also share an interest in it happening in a completely different situation.

HUO | A museum?

MB | I don't know about a museum, but a self-constructed situation or more informal situation that would be more in the tradition of performance and less in the tradition of opera.

JB | There would be the possibility of the different acts happening on different dates, too. Are you still thinking about that?

MB | Yes.

HUO | You started venturing into films with shorter films and then it went all the way to feature films. Now when one thinks about the stage it starts with Manchester, a piece which is part of an evening, and then leading to a full-evening piece.

MB | There is certainly a relationship to working at a scale that becomes like a self-organizing system; at least for me there is a difference between working on a more provisional scale or even on a smaller scale. For example, the way we are in Manchester. I think the idea of expanding the work into a full-length opera starts to have that same kind of potential that the films we've done have in that the thing becomes larger than you are and the thing itself starts to drive it and make its own demands. I still find that very exciting. I don't know how healthy it is.

JB | If the piece gets bigger in scope, does the language become more operatic somehow? In the same way you could think that as the films got bigger they became more like filmmakers would make them. I think that had to do with the fact that they were shown in cinemas. If a piece like this got bigger it would become a little more conventionally operatic if you wanted to do it in opera, to be able to take it from one place to another fairly easily. Do you know what I mean?

MB | I would say operatic in the sense of being immersed in an enormous emotional arc. What does it mean to be operatic?

JB | That's not what I mean. I mean more with conventional forces in a conventional space.

MB | I feel if it is about being immersed, that can happen in a number of different contexts. But in terms of our working relationship I do think it takes some duration, it needs to be a durational piece that allows people to get outside of themselves. I think it's the kind of thing that takes time; it needs some scale and some duration.

JB | Yes. But there is not a desire to make it containable and repeatable in a conventional space.

MB | Only in the sense of me being a somewhat practical person. I understand why a house needs to do that in order to take on a project like this: they need to be able to sell tickets night after night or a couple of nights to pay for it. I understand why that's necessary but it doesn't particularly interest me to make a piece that's repeatable. That isn't that compelling for me.

HUO | It has to do with the economy of production.

MB | Yes.

HUO | So for you, if it happens once that could be it.

MB | Sure, yes. I suppose I could change. It's something I find very compelling about the performance discipline; it's something I don't have. The way night after night something changes suddenly and that becomes part of the experience for the performers, certainly, and for very dedicated fans of the work who go night after night.

JB | That, in a way for me, is what is so beautiful about live things in contrast to what we were saying before about how it only happens once: the fact that to do it again you actually have to do the whole thing, whereas a film you show it twenty times and nothing really happens differently. The viewer has a different experience.

MB | In the production of a film the performer often doesn't have an idea of the entire script or the entire piece and that can happen, right? Some actors don't even want to know; they want to know about their character and the situation that they're in.

[*later in Hans Ulrich Obrist's apartment in London*]

HUO | One of the things we haven't spoken about is your exhibition with Joseph Beuys, which is now going to Venice.[20] You told me earlier that you were not a Beuys expert and there was something unexpected about this sort of approach to Beuys.

MB | I was saying that I think that Nancy Spector's proposal to make the exhibition was at first mainly about taking works from the Guggenheim Collection and making a small conversation with them. I think as we both started to go through the motions of thinking about what would be included and what wouldn't and looking at the works they had and thinking about other works out in the world that might make more sense, we got into a dialogue about it. We both became a lot more invested in it. I guess what I was confessing before was that I don't think either of us are Beuys experts by any means and somehow to go to Berlin and make an exhibition like this felt a bit outrageous, to go to the place where Beuys is most revered. But along the way I began to learn how his presence there has changed over the years and how an exhibition like this is probably more important than we realized as a way of repositioning, or attempting to reposition, Beuys in a way that might bring a younger audience closer to it. So that seemed like the thing that was most at stake.

20 *all in the present must be transformed: Matthew Barney and Joseph Beuys*, Deutsche Guggenheim, Berlin; Peggy Guggenheim Collection, Venice, 2006–07.

HUO | To bring Beuys back?

MB | Well, I wouldn't be as presumptuous as to say that. It's more to do with the fact that Beuys is gone and the memory of his activity is carried on as much by a generation of art professionals as by the work, because in a lot of cases the actions are either not documented or they are not documented sufficiently: there is only a photograph or two of a lot of really important performances.

HUO | Also the videos are not really accessible?

MB | The video archive is, I think, becoming more accessible, but it's still very separate from the sculpture and it isn't, by Beuys' design, really meant to be shown in proximity to the object. I think what Nancy did in this exhibition was to take some liberties with that material and I put together a film program which we showed in a cinema nearby where it juxtaposed those video documents of his work, some of which were just newsreel clips, very fragmented coverage of his performances, with some videos of mine. I don't know. In a certain way it did feel like we were presenting something to a young German audience that they definitely hadn't seen before and I was sort of shocked that he wasn't more present in the minds of the people from a younger generation. The more you talk to people who were around in Beuys's time, the more you understand why. I think it has to do with his position as a pedagogue in the German academy. But on the other hand I think what you learn by going through that video material and looking at it is that there's a lot of humor in it and seeing that those documents really breathe a lot of life into the sculptures. It is more visible. I guess for me that was the discovery, just how important that film and video material is.

HUO | Another aspect that became apparent through the show is this whole idea that his work has always been associated with materials. If we think about felt and fat, it's almost like a personified abstraction that has accompanied his life as an artist throughout.

MB | Yes.

HUO | In relation to that it would be interesting to talk a little bit about your signature materials, Vaseline or petroleum jelly. It's not in every piece and in every drawing like with Beuys, it's not so much a signature thing but there is definitely a very recurrent use of certain materials. Vaseline in particular pops up at the very beginning of the work.

MB | I think that a strong similarity would be that in both cases the range of material comes from a kind of critical autobiographical moment. For me I think it has to do with the locker room. It has to do with the apparatus that one is surrounded by in the athletic world, of being armored in plastic. From the age of ten to the age of nineteen I was covered in plastic all the time. I'm talking about football padding, the shoulder pads and the thigh pads and hip pads and knee pads and the athletic tape, the extra foam pieces that you stuff into a place that hurts, the vinyl tape you put over the cuts so you can put your helmet back on without it hurting like hell, all of these things that really become prosthetic. They become an extension of your body.

HUO | And you basically had that non-stop from the age of ten?

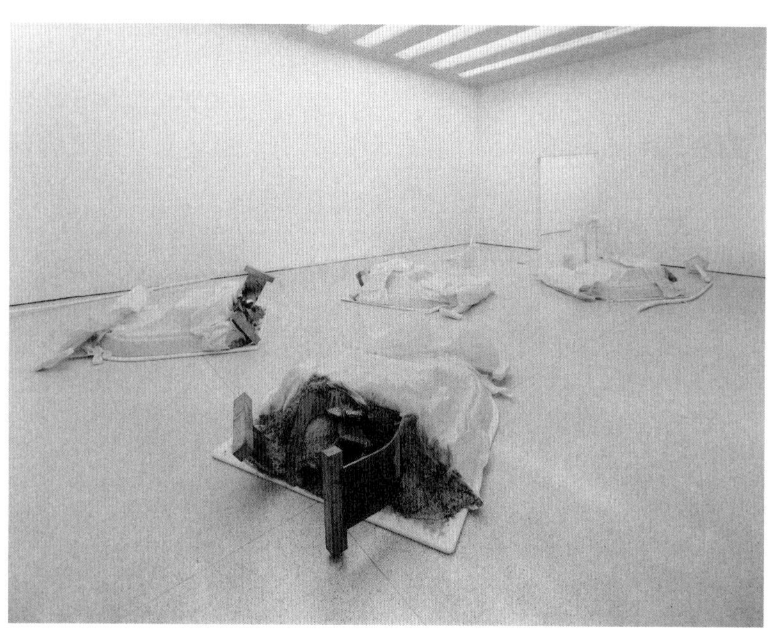

Chrysler Imperial, 2002
Cast concrete, cast petroleum jelly, cast thermoplastic, stainless steel, marble, and internally lubricated plastic
4 units at approx: 24 x 60 x 90 inches (61 x 152 x 229 cm) 1 unit at approx: 66 x 156 x 168 inches (168 x 396 x 427 cm)
Installation view: Guggenheim Museum

MB | Yes. It was at the center of my life, that relationship to athletics and to the training room and to the weight room and to all those things. I think when it started to feel like the only thing I could hold onto as an artist: the only way that I could begin to visualize making something was using this range of materials, this box of tools that I already had. Those were the materials that came forward: these plastics that were used methodically and those plastics belonging to the same family of plastics that are used internally as prosthetics and that sort of need for lubrication. An interest in resistance or friction, in the way you start building an apparatus around the body; it needs to move in a sympathetic way, it needs to slide across the body. Petroleum jelly was always around in the training room; it was always put in a place where something is rubbing, to take that chafe away. I think quite quickly it became formalized and that interest in materials expanded into a broader range of plastics and different ways of manipulating the plastic. Let's say my interest grew away from referring to its source or its native form and learning more about how that technology had developed and continuing to look for other plastics that could be used in other ways. So my dialogue with the material grew away from that.

HUO | So similar to Beuys, it started in childhood.

MB | Yes.

HUO | I think it was at your opening in Paris at the Musée d'Art Moderne when I spoke to your mother and she told me this extraordinary story that she helped you buy some Vaseline for the very beginning of the work.

MB | Yes. [*laughs*]

HUO | So that was for a very early piece?

MB | I don't know which one she was talking about, but I made pieces at college.

HUO | And then one can say these materials grew out of this athletic environment and became freed to some extent from this original significance; somehow they became free.

MB | I think so. I think they became the body, the frame within which this narrative could develop and from that moment the work became more and more narrative and these materials became the architecture for the story. I would say that over time, as the narrative changed the material changed, or let's say the material didn't change, the form changed. But I think also something I have always visualized with this material is that it could become anything or it could take any form, so in that sense its prosthetic nature hasn't ever changed: it's always been about its potential to be anything, in the same way that that plastic is used to build the body either outward or inward to help expand the body that way.

HUO | As you explained, these materials are a continuum. With Beuys however there is this idea of using a thing again and again, almost like what one could call a personified abstraction. I have the feeling that is a big difference between the 1960s generation and our generation. I don't read your use of Vaseline and petroleum jelly, for example, as a personified abstraction.

MB | I think I wouldn't either in that I think the things in my work that change less are part of the frame, they are part of this vessel, and the content changes. The content is what I think gives the work its face. On the other hand, that content is often borrowed, it's often borrowed from the place where the story takes place and although it's certainly abstracted, it's still appropriated material.

HUO | Like in the case of *Drawing Restraint 9* where it's borrowed from Japan and you are the visitor.

MB | So in a certain way the more consistent element of it in the work is closer to me but it's not the thing that gives a given work its face. So I can understand why you would say that those reoccurring materials are not necessarily the more frontal signature element in a work, in a sense. There is a body of content that sits in front of those sorts of things.

HUO | We could also talk about the vitrines. That's a link to Beuys which Nancy Spector draws out in her essay very beautifully, when she says the use of sculpture vitrines is an organizing device or organizing principle both in Beuys's work and your work. When did this enter into the work and what is the role of the vitrines?

MB | They function in a couple of different ways: they function first as a way of presenting the films so that they could be understood as objects, as belonging to the tradition of sculpture. It was something that was very important to me as these *Cremaster* chapters were being finished and being shown in art-house cinemas, to continue to position them within the language of sculpture. So I think the first vitrines I made were to house the film editions. I think it was a very conscious use of that device which turns everything into an object, that placement of something within a vitrine.

Essentially, the films were made as limited editions and sold that way and that's how they were financed, but what was presented and sold was a vitrine with an object in it and that object also carried the content of the film, literally. It had the content of the film on disc. That was important for me. And later, starting with *Cremaster 2*, I was using the vitrines to also make these character portraits, to take the primary characters from each story and make hybrid portraits between the characters. It often had to do with relationships between the characters. I continued to do that with *Cremaster 3* and *Drawing Restraint 9*, also. In fact those character vitrines from *Drawing Restraint 9* will be shown at Sadie Coles at the same time as the Serpentine show.

HUO | On the one hand there are the vitrines for the films and then there are the character vitrines in between, the kind of character blurs, where the vitrine becomes more like a sculpture.

MB | Yes.

HUO | So in this sense it is obviously very different from Beuys, where the vitrines are very often traces of actions.

MB | I am quite surprised that I would end up in a place where I am comfortable using vitrines, I have to confess, because I think that there is something about Beuys's practice which I was determined to avoid, which was for something to be extracted directly from the action and be allowed to be considered a relic. I am not opposed to it in his work, but I was opposed to it in my work in the sense that I really wanted a translation to take place from the use of that object in the narrative to the presence that it would have as a sculpture and not simply by framing it in a vitrine but for it to be manipulated. It was something that Beuys did do sometimes but those performance objects were often simply put into vitrines and exhibited as such.

HUO | So one can say that, in your case, the object is never the end point. It leads us back to the car we were speaking about before. Even the car which is stored somewhere can suddenly have a potential for a new life.

MB | Right. I think if it is, it just ends up in storage as a prop and it doesn't become sculpture.

HUO | Another aspect is the increased sociopolitical conscience in your work, looking specifically at *De Lama Lâmina* [2004/2009] with the eco-activist Julia Butterfly Hill. Obviously that is something Beuys had very strongly: he was the founder of the Green Party and initiated the *7000 Oaks* project. I knew Beuys as an activist when I was a kid and saw his lectures for the Free International University, which then led to the Green Party. It was very much the idea of the artist also being an activist.

MB | I never saw him first hand, so my relationship to all of it is totally secondary, but I think the work that resonates for me most is the work from the 1960s. The more political work in the 1970s was less compelling for me. That said, there are a couple of pieces I've made recently, *De Lama Lâmina, Drawing Restraint 9*, which do have a somewhat political program and it's something that up until that time definitely didn't interest me. I think the *Cremaster* project was very much about creating a hermetic space that didn't align itself with an external issue or with a direct view of the world that way. I think I would just say I don't think any of us have any choice at this point but to react in some way

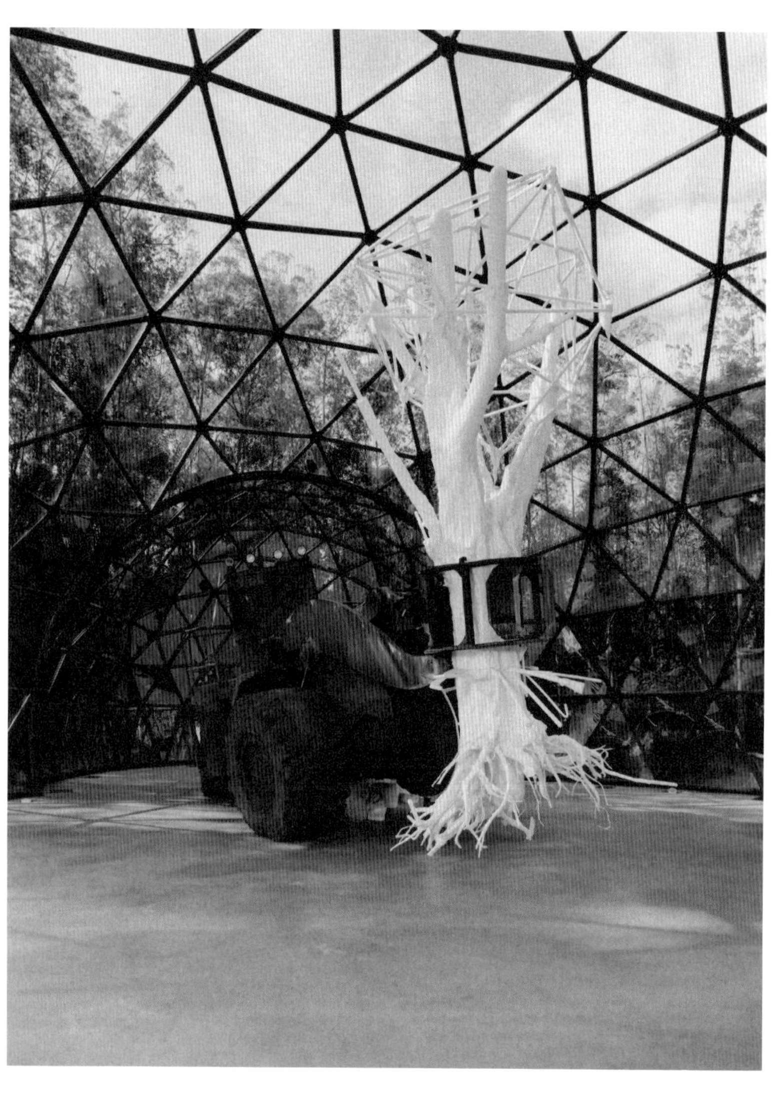

De Lama Lâmina, 2004/2009
Caterpillar 988 tractor, cast polycaprolactone, high density polyethelene, geodesic dome, and earth
Dimensions variable
Installation view: Inhotim, Brumandinho, Brazil

to the political condition that we live in. I think the way that it has seeped its way into my work is still fairly abstract but it's much more direct than I had been willing to allow into my work before this. In terms of the relationship to Beuys, I would say even with the most political work of his, he and his material and object-based presence never stopped being a conduit through which these external notions would pass and would transform and that's something that I feel very close to. It's the same way that I would identify my system: as a vessel that external stimulation and information, other environments, pass through. At the same time I would say that it also works the other direction in my case, which is my language seeks new environments and asks them to function like vessels that my language can pass through and transform. I think it works both ways.

HUO | So a bilateral kind of transfer?

MB | Yes.

HUO | Have there been any other artists you have a relationship with to the extent of Beuys? We spoke about Serra once before.

MB | I feel like I've learned a lot from Smithson and from Serra. It was interesting to see that Gordon Matta-Clark show recently and to realize how much that work affected me when I first encountered it as a student in a way that I didn't even remember. I think that also belongs to this sort of earthwork framework about a place. I don't know if somebody could make a whole exhibition about that relationship in the way that Nancy did with Beuys. On the other hand, I wouldn't have believed she could have done that a couple of years ago.

HUO | I think Smithson is becoming more important every day with climate change; our current world paradigm seems to be a Smithson moment. What is your relationship to Smithson?

MB | I think that the *Cremaster* ambition felt aligned with the earthwork ambition: to go out into the landscape and make a work that would integrate the entire landscape. In my case it was narrative, it was about going to a place and pulling the local mythologies into this form that would take place in that place, so the *Cremaster* chapters were place-specific works maybe more than they were site-specific. And the notion of the non-site, I think, is very relevant for the way I define the sculptures that come out of the *Cremaster* narratives; they are narrative sculptures that have been drawn out of that story that was place-specific. So they are similar to Smithson's displaced objects that way.

HUO | That's a very interesting link: the non-site.

MB | When do you think we need to leave?

HUO | In three minutes.

MB | Yes? [*laughs*] Let me just show you this because it's a fun image and then I'll walk you out. We are trying to capture reincarnation, literally, by filming the life and death of plants, not using a camera but using Magnetic Resonance Imaging. This is a one-micron section through a carnation and the beauty of MRI is that when it takes pictures it takes it of the real stuff, not of the shadow, of the water. So the idea is you can grow a plant and you can follow it in time-lapse using MRI but you are following the water in the plant.

HUO | So you see the life.

MB | You see the life. But then the plant dies, it degenerates; your eyes can't see it but the MRI still can. So the MRI enables you to see the water in space. Then you put in a new seed, a new plant grows, it takes in water from the environment; that water was literally the previous plant.

V Il Tempo del Postino[21]
Manchester International Festival, with Molly Nesbit, 2007

Part 1: Space for time

Hans Ulrich Obrist | So here we are in the early rehearsals for *Il Tempo del Postino* in Manchester, an exhibition in which every artist is not getting space, as is usual in group shows, but rather time. I was wondering if you could tell me about how the project started. As far as I understand, it has to do with the bigger picture, with you wanting to do a whole opera and this somehow being a step in that direction.

Matthew Barney | The first ideas I was working with were to do with another scene from this larger story and we ran into

21 *Il Tempo del Postino*, a group show at the Manchester Opera House, July 12–14, 2007, as part of the Manchester International Festival.

technical problems with that so I've elected to do a different scene. The piece you're speaking of is a longer performance using the text of Norman Mailer's *Ancient Evenings*. In this festival context there was the opportunity to take one scene and work that out and also for Jonathan Bepler to begin to put together what will be a through-composed, probably three- to four-hour-long piece. So we're at the very beginning of that project with this, so it's quite exciting for us to start to make that real.

HUO | I'm fascinated about how this project first began because it's most unusual. You got this phone call from Norman Mailer where he invited you to a book launch. It was almost as if he had given you a present.

MB | Yes, he asked me to read the first one hundred pages of *Ancient Evenings* and I believe what he had in mind was that a film could be made from that book. As far as where my head is at, I really don't want to make films right now. It really resonated for me as a script or more of a structure really. Those first one hundred pages follow the decent of a dying man as he loses the seven stages of his soul in the Egyptian belief system. So it offers a seven-act structure for this longer work. It was something like a challenge from him or a gift as you said. I think he felt that it was a narrative that I could relate to, which I certainly can. But it was also funny in the way that he let me off the hook, saying that I had to read the first one hundred pages but not beyond that, because he knows that I don't read very well. [*laughs*] Having worked together on *The Executioner's Song*, I think he understood that what we are talking about is an abstraction; it's not exactly taking the book and using it as a script. We're developing scenes that are not coming from that story, but rather using his narrative as a structure.

HUO | It also leads back to the discussion we had in London where you said you didn't feel much like making films right now. It's actually one of the rules of the game in *Il Tempo del Postino* that there is no film. This desire for a more unmediated experience is quite recent, isn't it?

MB | I don't think it is, in the sense that I've made performance in the past and I'd say that the beginning of the *Cremaster* endeavor was very much an extension of that performance language, in that everything was being performed for the camera in real time, nearly. I think as the first three films were made and the project gained more cinematic momentum, it changed and we made a couple of movies, by accident. Although the ambition became larger, the scale became larger, the failures were taken away somehow. I always felt in the middle of these film projects that there were situations that—if they could just be witnessed by an audience—were very resonant, nearly perfect situations, but what made them that way was the failure. There were positive takes and negative takes and situations that didn't have any takes. There were situations performed in real time from which, through the course of editing, you remove the failure and in a way take away something that was, in my opinion, very magical about it. It's something about the process of filmmaking that I'm wanting to step away from: that process of refinement and everything that happens post-production that kind of kills that moment. So it isn't new territory for me in that sense. I think that my filmmaking endeavor has always been an extension of a performance language. I was never educated as a filmmaker; it wasn't where I was coming from.

HUO | Your piece in Manchester will be about half an hour and it involves all kinds of different elements: a car, a bull and other live protagonists. How will these ingredients interact?

MB | To speak generally, it's a collision between two narratives: one is a Celtic-based narrative from *Cremaster 3* and the other is Norman Mailer's *Ancient Evenings*, an Egyptian narrative. Those two narratives are intersecting in what is something like a funeral for the *Cremaster* cycle. Using the language of *Ancient Evenings* and funerary practices from Egypt, you have one narrative that is describing the end of an entropic path, that's the *Cremaster* cycle and the other that has the hope for an afterlife, the Egyptian side. So these two narratives are in conflict in a way. There are characters from each. The bull comes from the Apis deity of ancient Egypt. However, the bull is not black as the Apis bull should be, it's a Scottish bull from the Highlands. The Entered Noviciate played by Aimee Mullins, from *Cremaster 3*, is carried in, veiled, dead and placed on top of the demolition car from *Cremaster 3*. There's a funerary priest, which is the character I'll be playing, which is a hybrid. On his head is an Egyptian dog, like Anubis the funerary priest from Egypt, his lower half is in the costume of the Entered Apprentice from *Cremaster 3*. There are some dancers that come from an Egyptian language, there are some New York City garbage men who are something like guards of this tomb that we're trying to create. There's a whole squad of musicians who are in IRA provisional military costumes, who come in and out of the scene and who are circulating around the house.

HUO | The last question for today was about the idea of the group show. When Philippe and I started out thinking about the idea of the group show where artists would be given time not space, it obviously also had a lot to do with this preoccupation and focus there has been in our generation, since the beginning of the 1990s, on time. So I'm interested in the different time notions in your work, but then also the togetherness: the idea of it being a group show and to which extent there are links to the other artists and their pieces.

MB | I'd almost be more curious to hear you talk about this in a way, because it's very different to some of the other group shows you've done, because of the focus you spoke about. There are autonomous pieces being performed one after another and I think that your program has been more about overcoming the standard architecture of the group show. Does this feel very new to you in that way? It certainly is as an evening of showcases.

HUO | It feels very new. Because the visitors are not moving through the pieces. They sit and all these different moments will pop up, almost like a pop-up book. What is also maybe new is that it's a different constraint, a different rule of the game, which produces very different work, which makes it different from any kind of exhibition with space, which is about showing or presenting a work. Here it is really about everybody producing a new work, which has to do with the very specific parameters of the place here. It produces work that otherwise might not have happened and I think that's also different from a group show, which normally brings together work the artists would do anyhow.

MB | I haven't been in a situation like this in a long time, since *documenta* in '92 and those first biennales I was involved with, where everyone is more or less producing new work for a show and they are allotted a certain amount of space.

HUO | You've met many of the artists in the show before and it also raises the issue of our generation: many of the artists in the show, as well as Phillippe and I, all met each other around fifteen years ago. Is there a lot of dialogue still going on, as in the 1990s, or has that shifted into something else?

MB | I don't know. I feel a little retarded in terms of that kind of dialogue. I have been involved, over the course of ten years, in these projects that took two or three years to do. I would disappear for two or three years and then come back and try to re-enter a dialogue. You're three years older, you've been away and you haven't been a part of it, so I guess I have an odd relationship to that. At the same time I think there is a familiarity with this group of people, which means that there's a certain amount of trust, which is important. I think we also trust you, which is important. I certainly wouldn't get involved with something like this if I didn't feel that way.

HUO | There are a lot of different positions within the show, but there is one thing that I think they have all shared is the preoccupation with time. Edward Lifson says that homogenizing forces of globalization also attack time, whilst in many of the practices we have a big variety in time.

MB | As much as I'm feeling slightly negative about film-making at the moment, one of the exciting things about it is that it has a momentum that has to do with the number of people involved, the scale of the thing, the momentum that the narrative starts to have. It starts to make its own demands and drive itself and have its own ego: that is exciting and liberating. I think that affects the project down to the organization of the scenes and the duration a scene has, it starts to decide for itself how long it needs to be, so I never really feel I'm making that kind of a concrete decision about how long something is going to be.

HUO | That's fascinating. So it's almost like self-organized time?

MB | I think it has to do with the notion of performing scenes in real time and not necessarily thinking about it cinematically or about how you'd set up the camera and the lights, all those economical questions that filmmakers need to think about, but rather setting up situations, performing it from beginning to end and shooting it. What you get is what you get. Hopefully you can afford to have a couple of cameras rolling so you can have multiple angles, but then accepting that that action has its own duration and it'll take as long as it needs to take.

HUO | That's a great motto: It'll take as long as it needs to take!

Part 2: On the terrace

HUO | One thing we didn't speak about in the first interview here in Manchester was something that Molly brought up: the question of whether there was any kind of link to vaudeville.

MB | I think the works I've made that involve Harry Houdini have always felt a connection that way, thinking about the sort of duality he had between a theatricality and a more hermetic practice. That was something that started to give some of the first narratives I constructed a structure. I'm

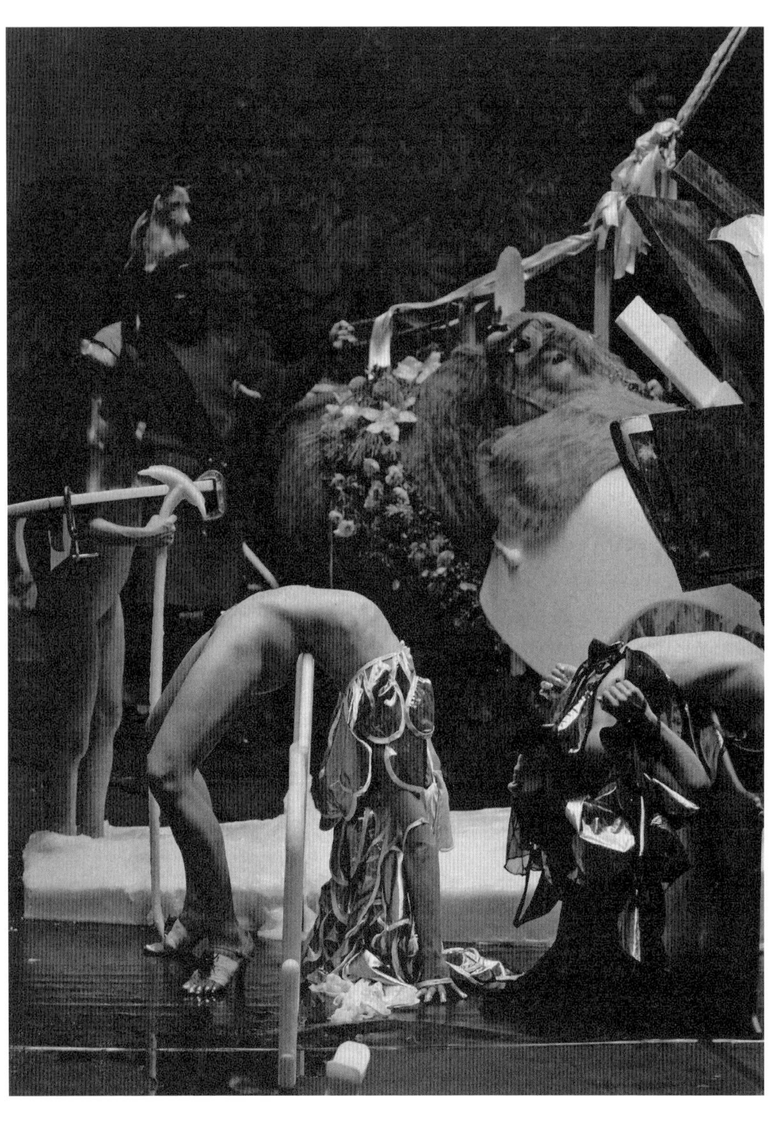

Matthew Barney and Jonathan Bepler
Guardian of the Veil, 2007
Performance still

still interested in that duality, but I don't think I'm dealing with that in a very literal way anymore.

Molly Nesbit | The reason I brought it up was not so much because of Harry Houdini, but when I put your piece and the Harry Houdini element in play it works. You produce the magic act: there's a ventriloquist, there's singing, there's a little bit of dance, there are puppets. It's a variety show and that's interesting because it's an old-fashioned way of presenting something to an audience and it's a repeated kind of performance. The audience keeps changing so the performance has to change. There was something that was kind of cool last night about the way in which the audience was there and in it and close. It's really different to the normal art experience, it's certainly different to making a *Cremaster* where you aren't personally in touch with the audience the way you were last night. In essence, you held your performance in the zone, which had a lot of talent in it of different kinds and yet it was so removed it was as if we were down in the bottom of the pyramids somewhere with no light. Then the curtain went down and that was it. So maybe the thing to ask you about would be the way that time kept extending as you worked at the piece: how did you arrive at that duration?

MB | We actually talked about that in the last interview. Duration becomes kind of intuitive at some point for me. It's not really possible for me to engage in a game or a recipe where you're given *x* amount of time to do something. I have to start something. It's the same way when I'm cooking: I can't follow a recipe, I have to just keep adding things until it tastes right. This here feels more or less like one of the scenes I've made on film before, but is a way of exercising that in a live situation, which is something I've been wanting to do for a while.

MN | It's a question about thrill. There are these points in your piece, narrative moments, like where the fist comes out for example, where it's kind of a thrill and a chill at the same time. Did you think about theatrical thrills and chills coming, narrative points, or places where time would stop a little bit?

MB | Sure. I think I've always had that relationship to violence or humor or things that I've used in the past or graphic sexuality. I think it's functioning here in the same way. It releases pressure, it suspends time as you said. I think these things are necessary. I also think that they become portals. I think when something puts the piece in a momentary suspension, then something can transfer from one character to another. For instance, that moment at the end where the character Tah's hand comes out: for me that's a kind of transfer from the bull to that character and for me those two characters are very related.

MN | Why didn't you take a curtain call with everybody?

HUO | That's interesting: none of the artists wanted the orthodoxy of the curtain call.

MN | It was a disappointment from the audience's point of view because there was nowhere to clap in a generous way for the whole thing. You might want to think about it again in terms of the dynamic coming from the audience: you need to give people a way to express themselves. A good audience will give a lot, but because they expect to be able to give it at the end, they save it for the end.

MB | The way that Jonathan and I have been thinking about this piece, it's been more about moving through the house and leaving. It's more about running over the audience than accommodating them. Originally we were talking about bringing the bull into the lobby, down the stairs, through the audience and onto the stage and we couldn't pull that off from a health and safety standpoint. But the movement of the musicians through the hall, down the top deck, down the second deck to the floor, and at some point we were talking about having them go onto the stage and out with the bull and everybody would essentially go from one end of the house to the other. So things changed, mostly because of the health and safety restrictions. We had a limit with how many people we could put on stage with the bull.

MN | Did you get any energy from the audience? At a music concert, for instance, the musicians talk about that all the time: whether the audience comes or goes, feeds or doesn't feed from what happens on stage. What about that factor? It's something new for you, isn't it?

HUO | And also did it change over the two evenings? The first night it was a contemporary art audience, which somehow fulfilled the role of a contemporary art audience: nodding and not really applauding.

MN | They don't use their hands much.

HUO | However, the second evening it was a Manchester audience, not a purely contemporary art audience, and there was much more interaction taking place.

MB | Yes, I noticed that people were laughing at the beginning of the piece, when the character of the dog comes out. That was the first time I felt any kind of connection to the audience, but I think once the procedure starts on stage I'd say that I lose that connection completely.

MN | Can you see the audience through all of that?

MB | I could if I wanted to. I think you should ask that question to Jonathan, because I think the way he structured his music, which is very fascinating, he wrote a modular score, which will never be the same any two nights. The string players have a written score, but everybody else has a range of four or five possibilities. Each one of those moving squads has four or five different figures that they've learned and when he conducts them, sometimes he tells them which of those figures to play, sometimes he just tells them to play and then there's a squad leader who will hold up their hands and say we're going to do number 3 and they play it. So it's more about interrupting or adding. It's like the cooking metaphor. Jonathan is a very organic artist in that way; I'd say he's the most organic artist I know. So I think he's feeling that part of the space much more than I am.

HUO | When I met Douglas Gordon for the first time in 1990 said that the 1990s might well be the decade of a promiscuity of collaboration. You've been very promiscuous in your collaboration all the way, yet you also have a continuum. Is this current decade, the 2000s, another decade of promiscuity of collaboration and how is this changing for you personally?

MB | Well, the collaboration with Jonathan Bepler specifically is something that works very well. It brings us both to a place that's very healthy, that's slightly away from our own individual position. I don't know in general about the decade! For me, even with some of the larger films and ambitious projects, it's still important to keep working on a grass-roots level, as crazy as that sounds. It is that way in terms of the relationships I have with this family of people who I've worked with for a long time. For example, I was very uncomfortable having to work with a professional production company in Japan. It was completely alienating for me. I work mostly with people who have plastic art experience rather than filmmaking experience. When it starts to become industrial it doesn't feel right to me.

VI In the Studio
Long Island City, with Julia Peyton-Jones, 2010

Matthew Barney | The core of the show at the Schaulager in Basel[22] is a conversation between sixteenth-century painting and works on paper and the *Drawing Restraint* series.

Hans Ulrich Obrist | Where were the sixteenth-century paintings sourced?

MB | Mostly from the Kunst Museum and a lot of the works on paper are from other places, but it's from the region. I think the idea was that the conversation would be with that area. I think where Neville [Wakefield, curator] started was with this idea of the Stations of the Cross and running that story in parallel with the *Drawing Restraint* story and kind of comparing two narratives that have a body that's

22 *Prayer Sheet with the Wound and the Nail*, Schaulager, Basel, 2010.

in an extreme position at the center. It was nothing more, not forcing it to be any more than this relationship. Then it grew and these more secular pieces that depict torture and the figure in an extreme position were included, so it has become a kind of culmination of these different works from that period. Then I'm making a work, *Drawing Restraint 17* [2010], in which I'm replacing myself essentially with a teen-age girl, a professional climber. She appears out in the fields outside of the Gotheanum, outside of Basel. She's walking through the fields of cherry trees and she's carrying this bronze shovel, which is an abstraction of the Gotheanum powerhouse, and she eventually comes to a place in the field where she starts digging. She digs a hole and this begins to inter-cut with another scene in an institutional space and you don't really know where you are. There's a group of art handlers and they're moving these pieces of rotten wood in different configurations and I'm there directing them, asking them to move them into this configuration and then changing my mind and then moving them again and finally we arrive at this pentagonal configuration.

Julia Peyton-Jones | Are there any symbolic reasons why it's pentagonal?

MB | Well it's certainly been an active form in my work and I think in regards to the show: the relationship between the armature and the body, the crucifix and the crucified body. I think that there's a moment when it starts to go there and then it retreats back to a form that's more de-centralized. So while they've been moving them around, pieces of this rot-ten wood are falling onto the ground, so at a certain moment the conservator comes in and she sits down and unwraps the piece and tries to glue the bits back on. She leaves and as the glue is setting, the pieces start falling back off. So the

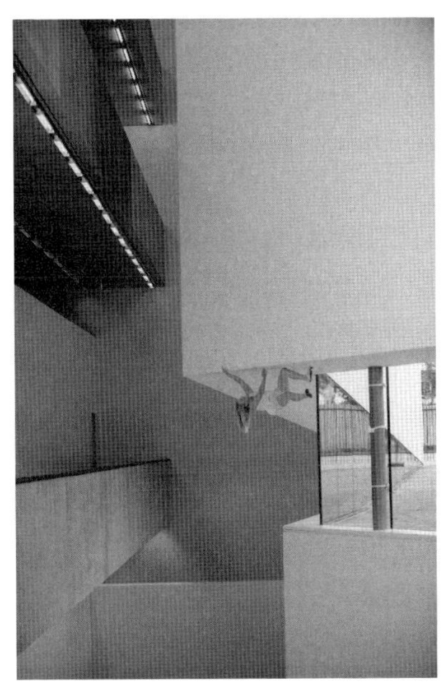

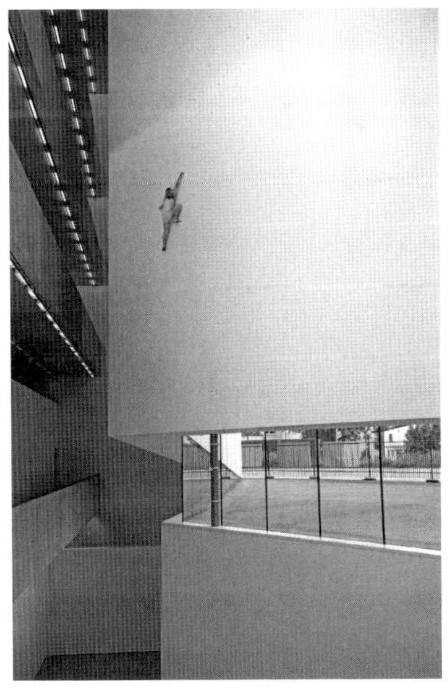

Drawing Restraint 17, 2010
Production stills

job isn't done properly. Back at the Gotheanum, the girl has abandoned her hole and she's got onto a tram and is riding in towards Basel. She's looking out at the landscape; she has let her braids down. She arrives outside the Schaulager, goes inside, climbs over a railing and walks along this window ledge. She looks up onto the wall and there's this climbing route that goes up quite high, about six stories high. Beneath her you see the rotten wood formation, which they'd covered with plastic sheeting after they had finished. She begins to climb up. She climbs freely with no protection all the way up to the top and when she gets to the top, she hesitates as she reaches for the last hold. She reaches for this last hold and the wall breaks at the top, and she falls back and she falls down through the atrium. The shot decelerates and her speed goes from a normal speed to moving very slowly. Then it moves into a close up of her body hitting this plastic film covering the wooden object. There's a kind of cross sectional view, where she enters the top of the frame, hits the plastic, then you lose her for a moment and she passes through the wood. Then underneath the wood you start to see her body push through the plastic where it is stretched thin and becomes clear and then it tears. This is where the film ends. [*pointing at an illustration of a Hans Baldung Grien painting*] This painting will be hanging next to *Cetacea*, a sculpture from *Drawing Restraint 9*. [*pointing at a second painting by Hans Baldung Grien*] This picture will remain in the Kunst Museum and a drawing that I've made will hang next to it.

JPJ | And what is the title of this?

MB | *Death and the Maiden*. At the end of this space there'll be a pile of earth that the Maiden dug from Goetheanum with the bronze shovel.

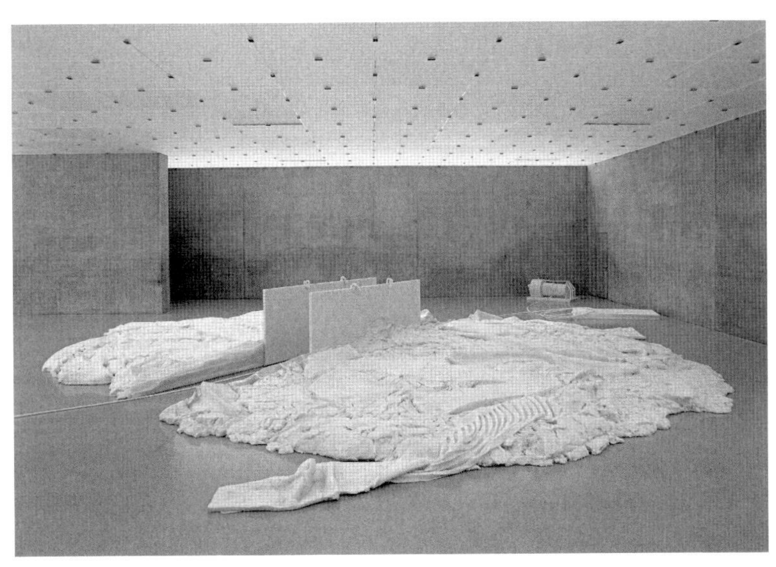

Cetacea, 2005
Cast polycaprolactone thermoplastic, self-lubricating plastic, vivac
(Height x diameter) 34 1/4 x 480 inches
Installation view: Kunsthaus Bregenz, Austria

JPJ | It's a very moving story.

MB | Simple, but I wanted it to be like a fable.

HUO | This connection to Rudolf Steiner is beautiful. Is this the first time you connect to Steiner like this?

MB | I think so.

HUO | Beuys was obsessed by him.

MB | I think that Beuys certainly led me there. I felt that replacing myself with a teenage girl was a nice place to start the story.

JPJ | Was it difficult to find her?

MB | No there are a number of these competitive climbers out there in this age range. In fact she's older than some of them, some are 14 or 15 and I mean they're just beating everybody. It's sort of like gymnastics, you know that age when their strength to body weight ratio is at the right place for something like this. They do this sport climbing inside, on these rock walls.

JPJ | And at what point are you at with all this?

MB | We start filming Monday; everything is pretty well coordinated. She'll perform the scenes, the climb and then we'll have this stuntwoman do the fall.

JPJ | I'm completely intrigued to know how she falls. How does it work?

MB | She falls onto an air bag.

HUO | But it's a real fall?

MB | Yeah it's a real fall. There's a danger involved, I mean you have to be trained to fall onto an air bag, you can't fall on your head. You need to know what you're doing.

JPJ | And no bouncing?

MB | Well, you need to fall flat onto it so your body weight is spread out, and the airbag folds up over you.

JPJ | Oh I see, I thought it was like a trampoline.

MB | No, no it kind of sucks you in. These are the drawings here. One of these will hang next to the piece in the Kunst Museum.

JPJ | What do you draw this with, because it's as if there's quite a rough pencil on rough paper?

MB | It's a paper that's mounted directly on aluminum, so it's quite a hard surface and the pencil is just a drafting pencil.

HUO | Is drawing a daily practice?

MB | No, I mean it is in terms of notation, but drawing like this I can only do every once in a while.

JPJ | Because this is very much like the finest tapestry. It's very, very precise.

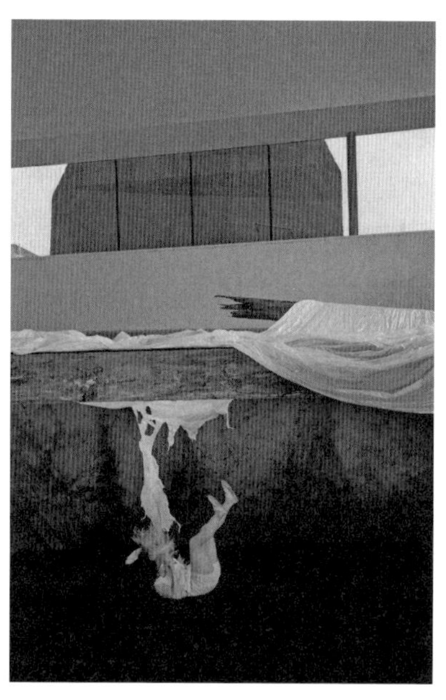

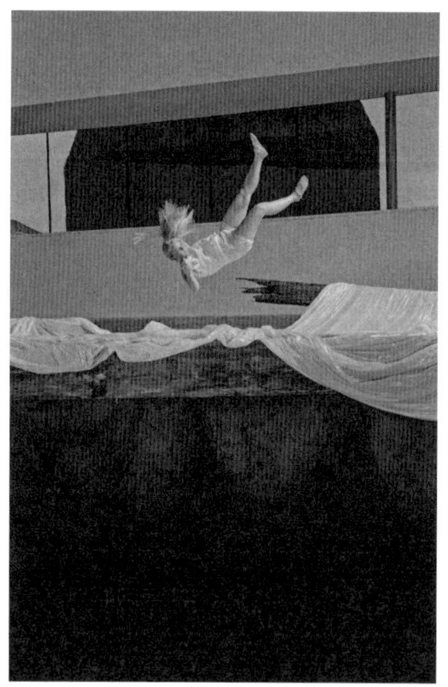

Drawing Restraint 17, 2010
Production stills

MB | It's becoming like a meditation for me; I think that's why I can't do it all the time. I can only do it when there's nothing distracting me. I couldn't do it in this environment for instance; I'd have to do it somewhere else. Airplanes are perfect.

JPJ | Really?

MB | Yeah you can't leave.

HUO | So you draw on the little table?

MB | Yeah, yeah.

JPJ | So one drawing equals one long-haul flight.

MB | No, it takes more like two transatlantic flights.

HUO | It's exciting, so *Drawing Restraint* is like the umbilical cord since the Serpentine show and continues and continues, and then parallel to that is Detroit. Is there anything we could see about Detroit here?

MB | Yeah, I could show you a couple of parts here. You know we filmed a prologue to the next act in Detroit in December and that's nearly finished. I can show you a rough cut of that but that's like 30 minutes long, so I don't know if you have time for that.

HUO | Oh, it would be wonderful.

[*walking around the hanger*]

MB | [*looking at a working drawing of a location in Detroit*] We are planning a scene on the Detroit River at the remains of an old steel mill, which made body steel for the automobile industry. The audience will encounter this site by walking up a long ramp. When they get to the top of the ramp they look down into a pit that looks like a recent excavation. And in there are these five towers that look like medieval casting cupolas from an old foundry. Smoke and fire will be coming out of the tops of the towers and a bunch of workers will be loading the material into the cupolas. In a scene inspired by the myth of Set, Isis and Osiris, the remains of the Chrysler Imperial from *Cremaster 3* is cut into 14 pieces and thrown into the cupolas and melted down in the furnaces. The five furnaces are opened and there's a flood of molten iron that moves right towards the audience who are all standing looking down into the pit. The pit fills up with iron and there's kind of a terracing system that eventually leads to an investment of the pit in this form. [*pointing at a silicone pattern for the iron cast*] So this object is then cast from the remains of the Imperial, and the new form is the undercarriage of a pristine '67 Imperial.

HUO | It's like an organic system, they are like organs.

JPJ | Or some kind of Pompeii, like a ruin . . .

HUO | It looks like an ancient city.

MB | And if you imagine this as a casting, it would be upside down and because of this terracing system it's a little bit like the bell-casting scene in that film by Tarkovsky, *Andrei Rublev* [1966], where there are these multiple sources leading to this one place. So there'll be a big iron flake as a result of that, which would be the reservoir that feeds the mold. As a casting there's this abstracted undercarriage, which is somewhat articulate and then there's this purely abstract flake that will be a really massive piece of iron. The flake will have the impression of the earth beneath it. I don't know yet what I'll do with that object.

HUO | That's even bigger than the piece you put in the jungle in Brazil.

JPJ | But Detroit is somehow perfect for that.

MB | Yeah, another big useless item.

HUO | So we need to go to this, what is the date?

MB | We have to block two days because we cannot do this in the rain because the iron will explode.

HUO | But why Detroit?

MB | It's where this car comes from ...

HUO | So to go back to the origin.

JPJ | And also it has such a funny feel about it now. I mean as a non-American this was a great focal point for industrialization and it produced so much of what we take for granted today and now it's so abandoned and sort of defunct. It's a very poignant symbol.

MB | I think what's really interesting about this place is that Ford did what he did there because all of the minerals he needed were there. So you really feel these levels of history there. Like a pre-historic one, that's produced all these minerals. There's a big salt mine that's beneath the city of Detroit. Actually, one of the reasons I went to Detroit first was to look at that mine. So I'm wanting this piece to have that feeling that Detroit has, which is that you can sort of see the strata of histories there. So it's not just that twentieth-century layer of extreme success and failure, but there are a number of other levels visible.

HUO | There was the idea to do Poland I think and there was the idea to do Manchester. But now it's Detroit. Is there a chronology?

MB | I mean the second and the third act are somewhat interchangeable, but I wanted this story to be told in order, unlike the *Cremaster* series, so I started looking at other locations, anticipating other acts, but it was important to me to do the second act after the first act. I went to look at a mine in Poland and met the owners. They were very enthusiastic. Jonathan and I developed a whole piece around that mine. We were just about to move into pre-production and we ran into problems I believe with the unions, basically to do with safety, about bringing a live audience into a mine and the possibility of an accident and what that would do to them. So after Poland I thought I should try Mexico. In Mexico it was the same thing. We developed a script for that location, which included a scene in the Crystal Cave of the Giants, where there are these enormous crystals that are 120 feet long, they're outrageous, like tree trunks. But it sounds like they're going to seal that chamber off. I think what happened is that as oxygen enters, the crystals will eventually go opaque. This has just been a huge burden for the mine because they were just mining lead there and knocked a hole in the wall and found this thing. Now every geologist in the world wants to come and visit it and they have to administrate it. That didn't work and so then we went to Detroit to see the mine there, discussed things with that owner for eight months. But while this mine conversation was dragging on, I started exploring other possibilities around Detroit because there are so many of them. I started speaking with the people who run the Rouge, which is the factory that Henry Ford built as the first vertically integrated assembly line. It's now a Russian steel mill. During those discussions, the idea was that this performance was going to happen within their assembly line. We would divert one crucible of steel and take it to another place and pour it into the ground, which was super exciting. At a certain point we were given approval, but then the economy fell again and they fired everybody from the CEO of their North American branch. So that proposal died. I got very obsessed with this, I thought I've got to make this sculpture; I want it to take place in this functioning factory, so how can we do this? They told me no, but the person in the PR department told me, "look the answer is no, but you shouldn't stop working on this because if you keep at it, it could happen." Which was the wrong thing to say to me. I spent a whole year working on it and finally in January the new CEO, he's a Russian guy in Detroit, called me and just said, "you gotta stop, no means no, please stop calling me!"

HUO | So what will happen after Detroit?

MB | I think we're going to do part 3 here in this studio. Then use the river.

HUO | Do you already have a script for part 3?

MB | Yeah I can show you the storyboards.

[*watching footage of the performance*]

HUO | So that functions like a trailer.

MB | I feel it's more like a piece of evidence. You'll see it establishes a crime scene.

HUO | What is the piece in Detroit called?

MB | *Khu* [2010].

JPJ | What does that mean?

MB | It's the level of the soul in Egyptian mythology that corresponds to the sight. When someone dies, first their name leaves, then the vision leaves, then the power and the mobility leaves. The Khu is visualized as a glowing bird that the deceased would see leaving. This is a rough cut, particularly in regards to sound; we're still working on it.

HUO | And what is this?

MB | This is a catholic church you'll see later on in the piece, but it's completely surrounded by sewage treatment tanks. I mean up until about two years ago they ran services and it smells so bad.

HUO | It's absolutely extraordinary to see the film and then the water. This is astonishing, gorgeous. Who's that performing?

MB | It's me, sort of in the role of the Apprentice in the *Cremaster 3*. There are a number of these *Cremaster 3* continuities: the lead investigator ends up being played by Aimee Mullins who was the Novice in *Cremaster 3*. So at a certain point in the story she becomes Isis and the Apprentice becomes Osiris, and the extraction of the Imperial from the river becomes about the body of Osiris, which is then taken by the jealous brother and cut into 14 pieces and in this case thrown into the fire and melted. It follows that aspect of Norman Mailer's book where he draws on that core Egyptian myth of Osiris and Isis. Here you see the sewage tanks around the church.

JPJ | But why did they do that?

MB | Well, they built the church for a nearby car factory. The car factory shut down and then they sold the property to the city and the city turned it into a sewage treatment plant and they added more and more of these tanks until they surrounded the church and then finally the church just had to shut down.

JPJ | It must have been quite tough to film.

MB | You get used to it.

JPJ | What about Houdini?

MB | Actually, this has very much to do with Houdini. He died in Detroit. He performed his first bridge jump in Detroit off the Belle Isle Bridge, which is where this story ends.

JPJ | Remind us again what all that noise is again.

MB | It's the sewage.

JPJ | And how difficult was it to break through the bridge? That must have been a drama.

MB | It was a drama to organize. We built a whole section of the railing which would break away and then replaced it.

HUO | And was someone really in the car?

MB | It's interesting. When they send planes off an aircraft carrier they use something like a slingshot, a cable system that's powered by compressed air that takes up the cable really fast and sends the plane off with a lot of power behind it. So in this case we built a wooden ramp and just shot the car off without a person in it.

HUO | So there were no dummies in it or anything?

MB | No and the windows are dark. And then there's this interesting retrieval system they use where they have a chamber in the back of the car with a bunch of very thin cable in it and at the end of it there's a buoy. The car flies off and the cable flies behind it and when it its hit the bottom of the river they pull back the cable and the buoy floats to the surface and then they can pull it up from there.

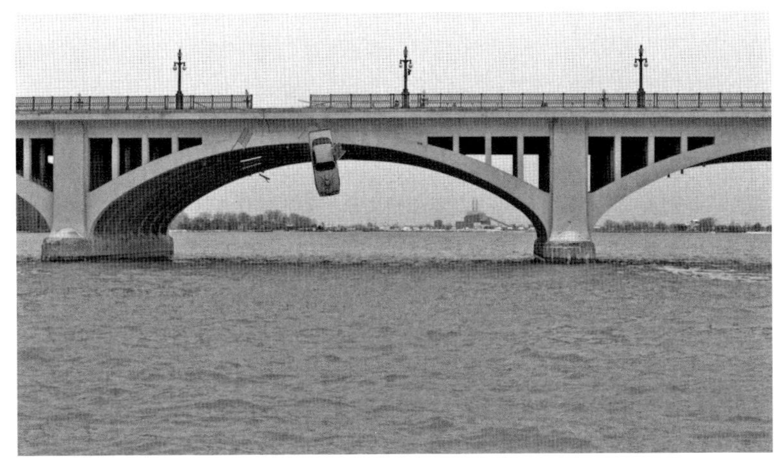

Matthew Barney and Jonathan Bepler
Sekhem, 2010
Video still
Video: Peter Strietmann

VII After the Storm
Mint Hotel room, Manchester, July 2011

Hans Ulrich Obrist | Hurricane! Matthew!

Matthew Barney | So how's it going?

HUO | It's good, yeah. Can you tell me what led you to go beyond exhibitions?

MB | You know, for me that was almost reactionary. At the time I was disgusted: I didn't want to participate any more in the way things were going. It was just the way that the art world was so bloated and market driven at that time. It was like you were never seeing the actual thing, you were always just seeing an image of the thing or being bombarded with the hype around it. It felt impossible to see anything that wasn't mediated in one way or another.

HUO | You were also saying at that time that our whole idea of gaining territory or getting out of the art world had somehow become a boomerang and that a new concentration was required.

MB | True, in a way, we got what we wished for, and it didn't work. Did you feel that way?

HUO | Yes, I felt that way as well, but I still believe in the Mailer idea that we should try to be most advanced yet build bridges. The last time we recorded was when we watched footage from Detroit in your studio.

MB | That would have been after we shot a brief scene there, but before we staged the live event.

HUO | So I know everything up until then and nothing since then!

MB | [*laughs*] OK.

HUO | There's just about one year that is missing that we need to catch up on. So since then there has obviously been the actual performance in Detroit, which Linda Yablonsky told me she'll remember her entire life because it was so intense.

MB | Yes, she's going back to Detroit. She's really connected to it I think. Detroit is like that. Not for everybody, but there is something very emotionally affecting about it, especially for Americans. I don't think you are able to see a place bottom-out economically like that very often in America. There is usually some kind of safety net. Detroit is past that point now, at least on an emotional level. It's not at the bottom, it's starting to redefine what it is, reinvent itself, so it's a particularly exciting time to be there and to meet the creative community there and see what kinds of solutions they are coming up with themselves.

HUO | I'm so glad to see you and it's great that it's after the storm on a quiet Sunday in Manchester.

MB | When do you leave?

HUO | Tonight. I wanted to go to Björk's show [*Biophilia*] today, but I couldn't wait, so I went the first night I was here. It was very exciting. When is your next show?

MB | In New York in mid-September.[23]

HUO | And what are you going to show there?

MB | I'm going to show three sculptures, mainly the piece that was cast in Detroit during the *Khu* performance, which is a piece called *DJED* [2009–11]. For the final scene we built a foundry on the location where the blast furnaces were removed from a derelict steel mill. It was a big steel mill that serviced the automobile industry through the mid-twentieth century. We dug a pit on this location and built these five furnaces and then poured twenty-five tons of iron into the ground to generate the castings for the *DJED* work.

HUO | That's one of your most monumental pieces.

MB | Yes, I'm really looking forward to showing it in this way, by leading off with the object. We probably won't exhibit

23 *DJED*, Gladstone Gallery, New York, 2011.

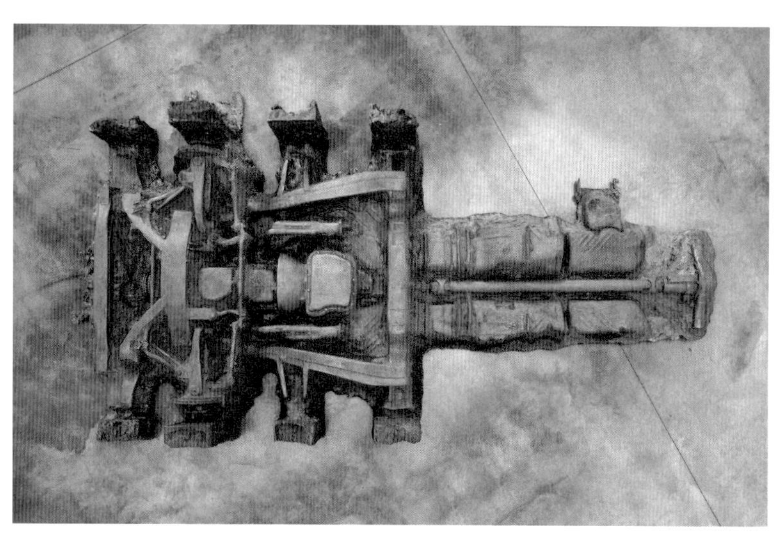

DJED, 2009–11
Cast iron and graphite block
20 1/4 x 406 x 399 inches

the film for another year, so in that way I'm changing the order. I want to start with the object.

HUO | It's your biggest sculpture ever?

MB | Yes, it's quite big. I mean, it's obviously horizontal, but it actually feels very horizon-like. It's very discrete in the way it becomes part of the horizon within the room. It's an interesting piece and of course it changes things to know how it was made. It's a very unorthodox way of casting something, like a medieval way of making a metal object.

HUO | Was the sculpture constructed or did chance play a big role? It seems pretty constructed; it's almost like a model.

MB | It does feel very model-like in a way, but the mold was made by taking the undercarriage of a 1967 Chrysler Imperial and cutting away parts of it, then burying it in sand and stone to form an abstraction of the Egyptian hieroglyph for the deity Osiris. One of the first moves I made in adapting Mailer's *Ancient Evenings* was to bring it into the American landscape and to replace Mailer's protagonist with a Chrysler Imperial. In the action in Detroit, the Imperial was recovered from the Detroit River and cut into pieces and then melted in this furnace. That 25-ton sculpture is the remains of the Imperial.

HUO | It's almost like Eduardo Paolozzi. Not in its texture, not in its cultural materiality, but in its shapes there is almost an evocation of early Paolozzi, a forgotten English Pop Art artist from the 1950s. He would distort elements of engines and so on, but it is very different.

MB | I would say that it's more abstract than it looks in this photograph.

HUO | It's both organic and geometric, according to your perspective. From here it's almost like a city, so it's also about micro/macro. So the film will not be present in the New York show, just the sculptures?

MB | And drawings. I'm also planning to make a playbill for the exhibition, a small booklet, which will include the libretto, as a way of communicating the narrative from the performance. I'm thinking this can provide a script for the exhibition, without illustrating the performance in images. It's an experiment. I think it's been a little bit complicated in the past to present an object as a sculpture when it's had the history of passing through the action, without being considered a prop or simply an ancillary product of the film or the performance. The intention has always been to make a narrative sculpture. So I'm curious to see how this works, to change the order in which the work is presented.

HUO | What I like about this is that one can all of a sudden say that the whole Detroit performance and action and the whole epic project has actually happened in order to produce this one sculpture.

MB | Yes, which it has.

HUO | In this sense the sculpture is the protagonist and it's charged by all these things that have happened. It's interesting that in the *Cremaster* series people thought the sculptures were props, even there they were often autonomous sculptures.

MB | Well, I think the program has always been the same. I'm an object maker, that's what I'm interested in. The same goes for my interest in performance. Performance for me has always been about the object, it's never been about theater. The program with *Cremaster* was the same. It was about creating a story, out of which I could make narrative sculpture.

HUO | So the exhibition will basically be this big sculpture in the middle, surrounded by drawings. Obviously we here have a situation that is post-performance and we see the mold and we see the cast, but it's something that you've constructed. You've constructed the lake or the pool, you've constructed the lead ways to the sculpture and then this edited car chassis, which looks like a city from certain perspectives. How exactly did this come about? Was it something that was in the center of the Detroit performance from the very beginning?

MB | I think that this form, which is called the Djed, is a compelling object in Egyptian mythology. On one hand it's part of the hieroglyph of Osiris' name, it refers to his backbone, possible to the tree that enveloped his body in the Nile. But I think what is more interesting is the speculation that has been made that the Djed column was part of a system that was being constructed by the Egyptians to electroplate an object in gold. Of course this is totally speculative, but in that way the Djed column is something like a capacitor. The object that was cast in Detroit is in the form of the Djed column. As the *Ancient Evenings* narrative continues, this desire to form an electromagnetic field will continue. That will be the core narrative that will take us through the end of *Ancient Evenings*: the attempt to control electricity that way.

HUO | The encounter with Norman Mailer was of importance.

MB | Yes. I am now working out ways of bringing Mailer into the piece as a character. Of course it's very difficult, he's not with us, but this is one of the things I will try to do in the next act.

HUO | The nineteenth century was so obsessed by history, which is somehow to do with the French revolution being the opposite of history. There was this great obsession with Egypt also. I was wondering if it was Norman Mailer that triggered your interest in Egypt or if it was something you had already.

MB | No, in fact, when Mailer first approached me about *Ancient Evenings*, my first reaction was that I'd already made this piece. *Cremaster 3* had already covered much of that: freemasonry, the Masonic connection to ancient Egypt, the building of the temple, the fall of the temple, etc. In a certain way I feel like I'm retracing my steps. I've just come back from Paris where I met with Bruno Racine and we're developing an exhibition at the Bibliotech Nationale for 2013.

HUO | That's the perfect match with New York.

MB | Yes, it's a very nice match with the Morgan Library. But this building in Paris, the Bibliothèque Nationale is interesting. There are some theories that it was built to the program of Solomon's temple. To what extent that's true I have no idea, but it doesn't matter.

HUO | We can ask the architect Dominique Perrault.

MB | Yes, it would be good to talk to him. But don't ruin my program! It doesn't matter if it's true or not, maybe it's better that I don't know. But what's more interesting is that that library owns a massive collection of Masonic material. One of Bruno Racine's predecessors was completely obsessed with the Masons. He was imprisoned for life as a Nazi sympathizer and his collection was confiscated and given to the library and the majority of if was Masonic. The library hasn't found a way to exhibit it, though I think I might be able to work with it. I've just learned this and I don't know how that will affect what I'm doing. What I'm planning to do is take material from the library's holdings and replace elements in my storyboards with manuscripts and rare books and so on. So on one hand it's a straight forward drawing show, on the other hand it will try to emphasize the relationship to narrative in the drawings by using some of this other material.

HUO | Will your books also be part of that?

MB | I hadn't thought of that, but they should be there.

HUO | A few days ago I was looking at the bookshelf with all your books on it. You've done a lot of artists' books.

MB | There are almost no catalogues, perhaps two.

HUO | You've successfully resisted catalogues! What has also happened since we spoke last was that your *Drawing Restraint* archive has entered the MoMA/Laurenz Foundation collection, which is like a new chapter.

MB | That's true, but hopefully it's not the end of something, but is rather putting the contents of an ongoing project into a more public housing. I very much want it to be an open archive and to continue to produce *Drawing Restraint* works.

HUO | Can we talk some more about the Detroit performance?

MB | The primary situation was that the audience was transported on a barge down the Detroit River. In certain cases they were seeing scenes from a distance, while in other cases they would disembark and have a more intimate view. This scene for example had a narrative which the audience couldn't really see, with dialogue they couldn't hear. They were watching it the way one would witness a crime scene from across the street.

HUO | And is there a crime?

MB | Well, in the second act you see that a gold Trans Am is driven off the Belle Isle Bridge into the Detroit River. This is where Houdini made his first ever manacled bridge jump. Later, in Act 3, the investigators at this crime scene are looking for something, and what they find is a shred of the James Lee Byars jacket, which the driver of the gold car was wearing. This is further down river from the Belle Isle Bridge.

HUO | That's also interesting because James Lee Byars was into Egyptian death cults. He is buried in Egypt. What are these?

MB | Snakes. They find them in James Lee's sleeve!

HUO | Are there snakes in Detroit?

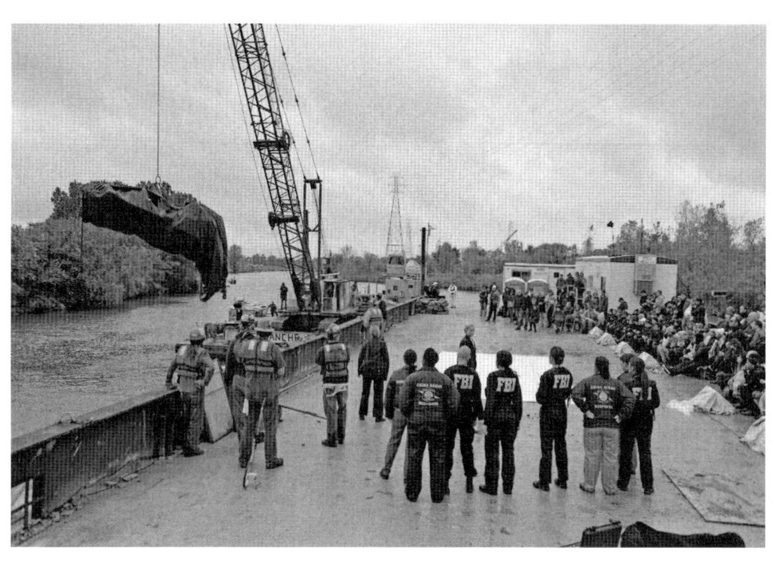

Matthew Barney and Jonathan Bepler
Khu, 2010
Performance still

MB | Sure.

HUO | Poisonous ones?

MB | Perhaps. These were not poisonous. Later in the scene, as the investigators board a boat to look in the river where the evidence was found, you can hear the approach of brass instruments. These are patrol boats and each one has a quartet of saxophones on board. They circle around the investigators as they look at this protrusion in the water.

HUO | Last time we spoke about the Detroit piece I asked you about the grand narrative, also in relation to Mailer's grand narratives. Yesterday I spoke to Adam Curtis, the visionary journalist and documentary filmmaker. He said that we're living in a very narcissistic age where everything is about emotional attachment to fragments and that within this we lack big stories, emotional narratives. I was wondering how you felt about that.

MB | It's an interesting question for me because I think these narratives are large and the related works are large, but the stories are made from fragments.

HUO | What is happening here?

MB | A team of investigators are craning an object out of the river and placing it on the barge where the audience is standing. The investigators unwrap the object and they realize that it's the body of Osiris and the mourning begins! [*laughs as shrieks and howls can be heard in the background*]

HUO | It's a bit like in Greece at Deste in Hydra with Elizabeth Peyton where you also had that coming out of the water thing.

MB | Yes, but on a much larger scale. In a way that was a rehearsal for this. I was already working on this story at that time. The thing is that those Egyptian narratives were rewritten in Greece. So there is a cult in Greek mythology around that fundamental Egyptian story of Isis removing the body of Osiris from the river. I think that that Easter celebration we were working with on Hydra relates to this narrative.

HUO | How did you make the film?

MB | It's done in a peculiar way. Basically all of the master shots are captured in one day, over the course of seven hours. Then close-ups were taken in rehearsals the previous week. It has been interesting to start to show this to other filmmakers because of this unorthodox process.

HUO | Will it be a cinema film?

MB | I don't know yet and I'm enjoying this uncertainty. So here is Isis. She is casting a spell and putting snakes into the cylinders of the engine block. Then she pulls her pants down, sits on top of the engine, and makes love to the Imperial, who is her lost love, Osiris.

HUO | Who is she?

MB | Her name is Aimee Mullins, she was in *Cremaster 3*.

HUO | And is the sculpture made by Aimee Mullins with the snakes also going to go into the show?

MB | No. It's melted.

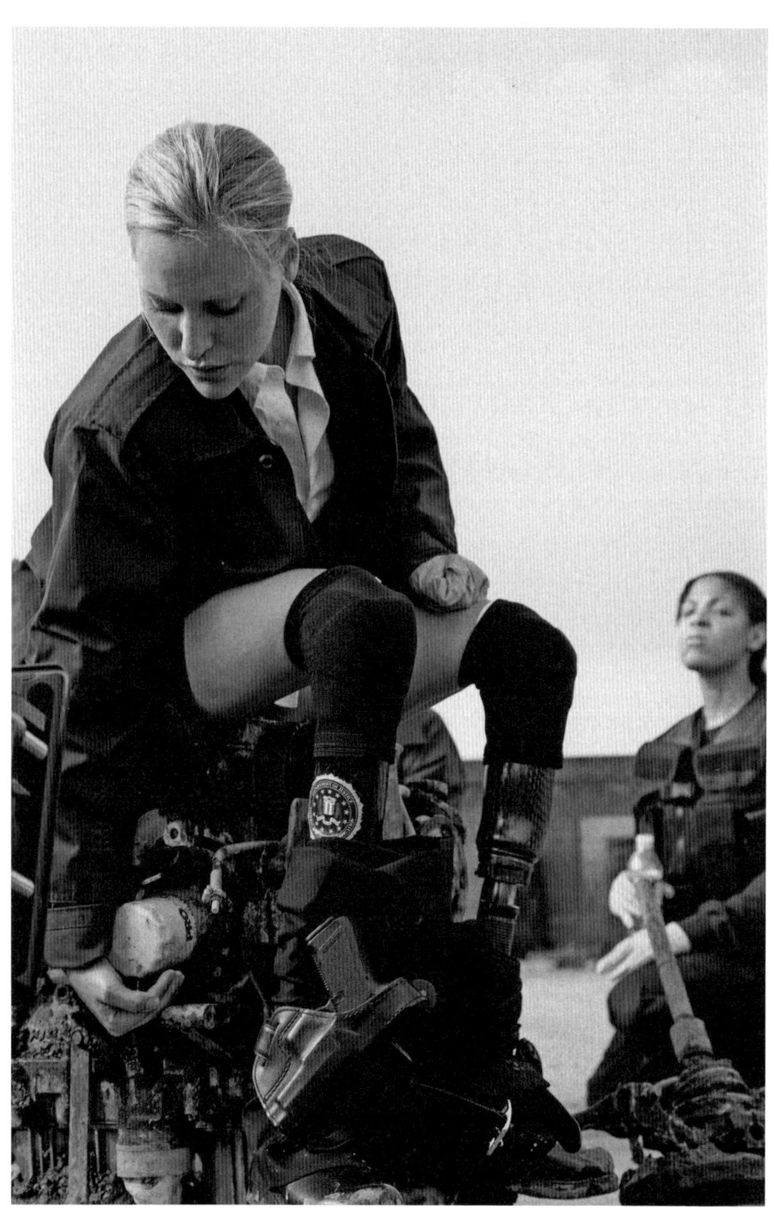

Matthew Barney and Jonathan Bepler
Khu, October 2, 2010
Performance still

HUO | Wow.

MB | So I'm going to skip a couple of scenes. The boat carries on five miles down the river and arrives at this location where one of the big automotive steel mills now stands derelict. These two guys are a manifestation of Set, who we saw earlier, when he killed Osiris by guiding his car off the Belle Isle Bridge. Now he is taking the body back from Isis.

HUO | So how long was the performance overall?

MB | Probably between seven and eight hours. [*laughs*]

HUO | And how long is the film?

MB | It's two hours and fifteen minutes, but we're only approximately half finished with the story.

HUO | How does the editing process work? How do you compress eight hours into two hours?

MB | Well, a lot of that time in the performance was represented by intervals where very little action was happening, where you were traveling from one place to another. You're seeing a lot in terms of narrative information in the landscape, particularly in Detroit, where it's very easy to see the layers of history in that landscape and to see the successes and failures of that city.

HUO | Has John Chamberlain ever been an inspiration for your sculpture?

MB | I always hated Chamberlain's sculptures because they felt so literal. But you know what, I saw that show recently in New York and I thought it was really interesting. Usually when work goes into that Gagosian gallery it just becomes bigger and its meaning doesn't change. In this case the sculptures became bigger, but they stopped being in the scale of the automobile, which made them more abstract and I think more interesting. So this scene is obviously more opera like.

HUO | Could one describe the whole performance as a sort of dislocated opera?

MB | Yes.

HUO | It's like what happened with your piece for *Il Tempo del Postino*, but over an entire city.

MB | Yes. So in this scene Set confiscates the Imperial and commands his crew to cut it into fourteen pieces. Here on top of the towers you have these five James Lee Byars characters watching over the cutting scene. So in the final scene the power has been overthrown. Isis has been taken hostage, the Imperial has been killed again by Set.

HUO | The vertical elements also somehow remind me of the melted atomic plants in Japan. Why James Lee Byars? We haven't really spoken about him before. Has he always been important for you or did he become important through that piece?

MB | I think Byars was always important for me in the way that his performance was very much about the object, but at the same time the object was often in drag, in the sense that it's trying to be something that it's not. These platonic forms guilded in thin gold foil, or simply painted gold . . . I think this uncertain relationship to the divine is accurate for *Ancient Evenings*. I also think his place in terms of American art-history is sort of similar to Mailer's *Ancient Evenings* in some way. Both are fundamentally American, but wrapped in a thin layer of gold from another culture.

HUO | And Byars was obsessed with Egypt.

MB | Yes, he died in Cairo and he had quite grand plans for an Egyptian burial, which never happened.

HUO | Did I tell you I went to the cemetery? It's the American cemetery in Cairo. There was a woman drying laundry on the tombstone and we had to ask her to remove it.

MB | I don't exactly know how to put it, but I think there's a way in which Byars captures a lot of different levels in *The Ancient Evenings*, from the fact he was born in Detriot and died in Cairo, to the point that his performance was object based, but he also captures this notion of failure that this story is trying to take on. I always loved about seeing a Byars exhibition that there was an object in the room that was gold-leafed or made of marble and there were velvet ropes around it and it was a very precious situation and he'd be standing in the corner in his gold lamé suit reciting Haikus or whatever he was doing, but it made the installation uncomfortable in the way that it was trying to be something that it wasn't. I always thought that was very beautiful. They are highly idealized situations, and idealized forms, and there is something very problematic about it in an interesting way.

HUO | He was always in search of the perfect object.

MB | I think in Byars's mind these things were solid gold and perfect platonic forms, but of course they weren't. They were never made in that way. The room was painted gold, it didn't have that kind of permanence.

HUO | This is a gorgeous film, congratulations. It's very different from all the other films. It's a city and this whole movement throughout the city.

MB | But in both cases, here and in Los Angeles, there's been something like this at the center of the piece, something that cannot be repeated, cannot be reversed. It makes it impossible for the performance to become a repeatable program. Somehow that's been important to me. The car can only be cut into pieces and melted once.

HUO | That was already the case with *Il Tempo del Postino* here in Manchester exactly four years ago, when we sat in the City Inn hotel, the same hotel we're sitting in now, only the name has changed, it's called the Mint Hotel. I didn't understand that at the time, but that was also something that couldn't be repeated. When it actually toured we realized we couldn't tour your piece, because the piece was gone!

MB | What was very useful for this final scene was the scene in Tarkovsky's *Andrei Rublev*, where a church bell is being cast in the medieval way. It has a similar feeling to this.

HUO | But there is also Andrei Tarkovsky's idea of the ritual. The casting of the bell is a ritual. The idea that we need twenty-first-century rituals comes from Tarkovsky. Who did the sound?

MB | Jonathan Bepler.

HUO | What happened to the rest of the cast metal?

MB | Pretty much all of the cast metal is part of the *DJED* installation. The furnaces were far too big to keep. There's a whole community out there of DIY iron casters who hold casting meets. They make their own furnaces, everyone brings a mold, they work together for a weekend, keeping the fire burning and metal melting. We donated the furnaces to one of these communities. For *Khu*, DIY iron casters came from all over the world for the performance and worked on this pour, which is the largest non-industrial iron pour that has ever been attempted with this form of casting. So they were completely psyched. It was like climbing Mount Everest for them.

HUO | Did you make one cast of this sculpture or several?

MB | Just one. There couldn't be another casting, as far as melting the protagonist of the story into the object. In the final scene there were streams of gold fluid, which were pouring down from five manifestations of James Lee Byars, who were each standing on top of 130-foot towers. It was beautiful.

HUO | So you did the James Lee Byars funeral that he didn't get in Egypt in Detroit!

MB | [*laughs*]

HUO | Having seen the cemetery I was really sad but now I feel better. He got his due.

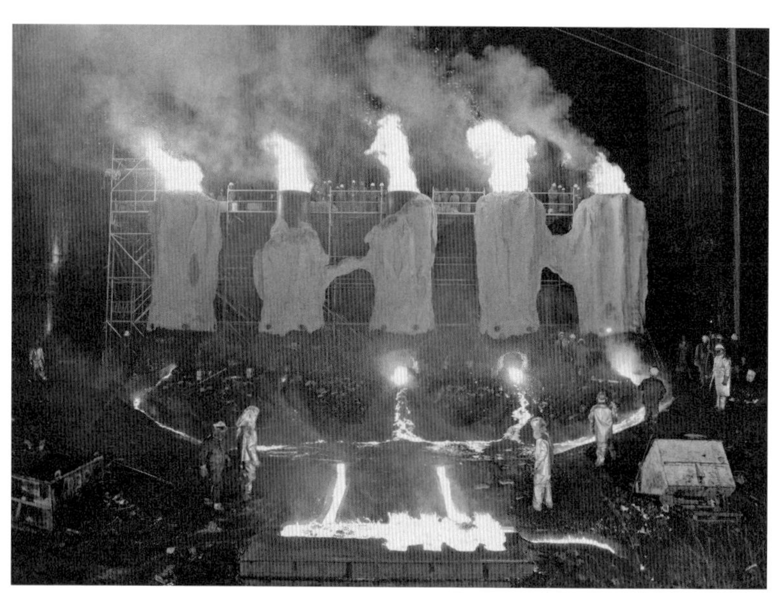

Matthew Barney and Jonathan Bepler
Khu, 2010
Performance still

MB | Fantastic. So now we'll go on to New York and make the rest of the story there. That said, I'm preoccupied at the moment with the ability this project has to generate sculpture.

HUO | So this is basically ready to be screened?

MB | Well, we still have acts 4 through 7 to complete, but this cut is starting to work well as a hybrid document of what happened in LA and Detroit. This part right now is an epilogue. The woman singing is Belita Woods. She was one of the P-Funk All Stars.

HUO | And what about the object we just saw?

MB | Those are actually called "abortions": crucibles of hot material that have to be dumped because the mold is not ready. You often see them lying around steel mills. They're too heavy to move. It costs too much to even move them so they just leave them. We nearly had to abort our casting. While we were casting it was raining like hell, and in a situation like that, water gets trapped under molten material, it expands and explodes the metal out of the mold. We had to evacuate the audience in the middle of the scene for fear that it would explode. Luckily this didn't happen. The audience saw the molten iron starting to come out of the furnaces but they didn't see the filling of the lower chamber of the mold. Quite a dramatic moment to have to leave. I don't think there was any loss of drama.

HUO | Where will the next performance be?

MB | In a couple of locations in New York.

HUO | Do you have any more film you can show me?

MB | Did I show you any of Los Angeles?

HUO | Yes, I saw that. So now we need to talk about the next chapter.

MB | I think what I'm interested in trying to do is to finish these site-specific chapters and finish the film in the New York locations. After that it may be of interest to take the literature of the piece and translate that to the stage. I'm hesitant to commit to anything right now because this has taken so much longer than I thought it would and I don't know how long the rest of this is going to take.

HUO | But that's not something new for you. With *Cremaster* you also didn't know how long it would take.

MB | But this piece is a collaboration, so it's different. It moves at a different speed. In principal I am interested in the possibility of expanding the performative aspect of this, on the other hand I'm so much more interested at the moment in the way this piece can generate sculpture.

HUO | The sculpture is a masterpiece.

MB | There's also a large bronze piece called *Canopic Chest* [2009–11].

HUO | Can we see that?

MB | I can show you some pictures of it as it was installed in the studio.

HUO | So the outcome of Detroit, or the production of reality to be more precise, is not only the very big pool and iron sculpture, but also a bronze piece.

MB | So what you see here is the whole bronze casting system, which is usually removed from a finished piece. These are the casting cones where the molten metal goes in. Here on the back is a large cone where the trapped gasses come out. Sitting on the top is a polished bronze piece. It still has all of the core pins on it that would hold the ceramic mold in place. It has a similar kind of rawness to the iron piece, but this was made in a proper foundry.

HUO | And this is also something that couldn't be repeated?

MB | This could be repeated. This is one of the challenges in making this exhibition. It combines two very different sculptural languages.

HUO | It's fascinating that something that cannot be repeated and cannot be rehearsed actually produces these eternal objects.

MB | These here are the lids to the four canopic jars that are inside the body of the piece. That form is the negative impression of the underside of the front end of a 1967 Imperial, but in functional terms, it is a canopic chest, a cabinet to house the four canopic jars, used in Egyptian funeral practice, to house the internal organs of the deceased.

HUO | Will it be put on a box?

MB | Not a pedestal. It sits on top of cast bronze timbers.

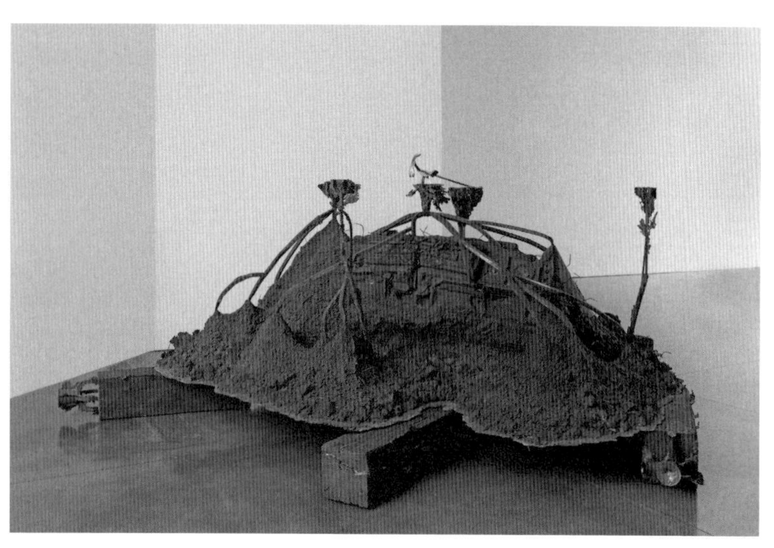

Canopic Chest, 2009–11
Cast bronze
73 1/2 x 165 x 243 inches

HUO | Joseph Beuys's basalt stone pieces were always put on the floor and they only found out recently that he'd actually wanted them to be on the wooden pallets. Udo Kittelmann told me that they've recently rediscovered these original wooden pallets at the Hamburger Bahnhof!

MB | So what happened? The institution thought that the pallets were just part of the storage?

HUO | Yes. This is incredible though. And it's big.

MB | Yes, it's bigger than this room.

HUO | So will your piece fit into the Barbara Gladstone Gallery? Will it be in both of the galleries?

MB | No, just the new one, the open plan space. But I'm taking the desk away and placing the canopic chest right at the entrance.

HUO | And then the big piece with the pool in the main space and drawings on the wall?

MB | Yes.

HUO | And what is this?

MB | This is a third sculpture, called *Secret Name* [2008/2011], which will be installed in a small gallery upstairs. It is made of cast lead, zinc, copper, and thermal plastic. The metals are nearly all corroded. There's a thing that happens when you put metals in proximity to one another in a corrosive environment. An electro-chemical reaction occurs, where

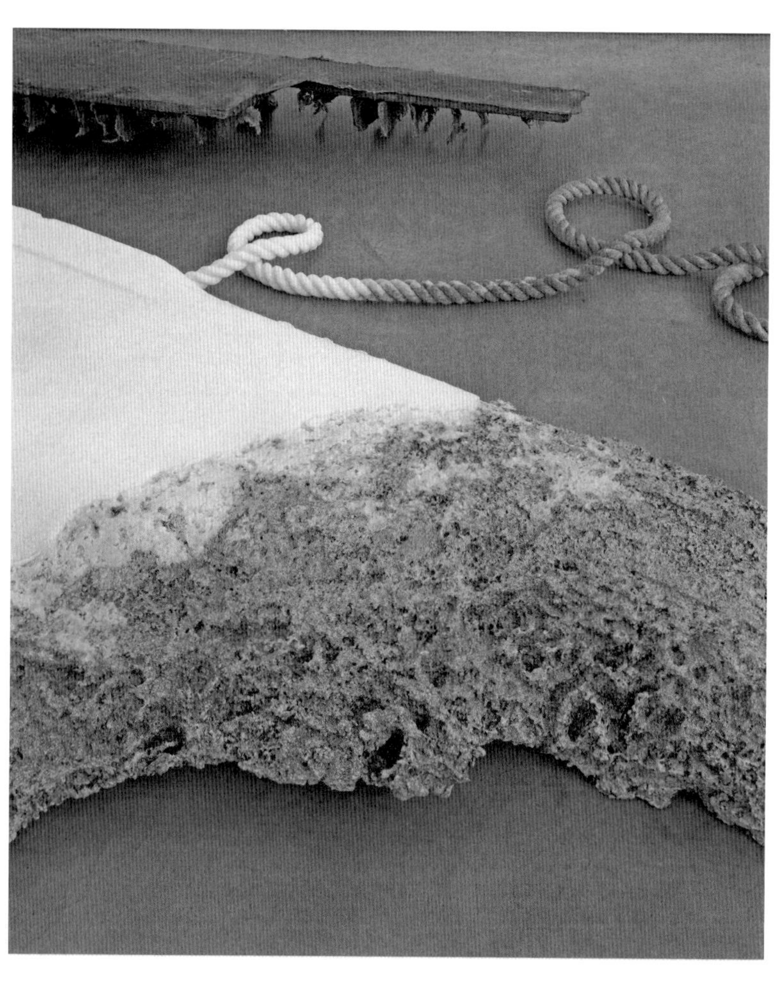

Secret Name (detail), 2008/2011
Cast lead, polycaprolactone, copper and zinc
21 3/4 x 179 x 128 1/2 inches

the inferior metal, or anode, attracts all of the oxygen, and it corrodes, while the superior metal, or cathode, is protected by the molecules it attracts. One solution is to introduce a third metal, which is inferior to both, as a sacrificial anode. This piece of metal will corrode, to save the other two metals, and can be periodically refreshed. So this piece, in a way, translates the narrative, in more electro-chemical terms.

HUO | So, what started here in Manchester in 2007 with *Il Tempo del Postino*, is a sort of post-*Cremaster* period. We have covered *Cremaster* in our interviews, and we've covered *Drawing Restraint*, but then obviously something has started which you are now in the middle of, which are these site-specific projects. You have been in Mexico, Los Angeles, Detroit and New York is still to come. That might then come to a conclusion. So *Drawing Restraint* continues, you've just had the latest book in the series published and on the other hand you're coming to the end of a chapter, but it doesn't really have a name yet. And then we have to talk about what is coming after that.

MB | One thing that has happened in the process, and I didn't expect this to happen, is that it has reactivated my interest in filmmaking. I think one of the things that interested me in creating a live performance was that I was disinterested in my filmmaking at that point. I think this is what we were speaking of earlier: this very strong desire to have an unmediated experience. I was tired of the editing process. When we made those *Cremaster* films for example, a ritual *did* take place on the set and the people who made those pieces were part of that ritual, but the people who saw those films were not. I think there was something in that process that never made it to the screen and that always disappointed me. So I wanted very much to bring people into that ritual.

HUO | Which you did in Manchester, in L. A., in Detroit.

MB | But I've been documenting this and I've ended up with a kind of hybrid film, which I'm interested in. It's neither a documentary nor is it a piece of straight-forward cinema; it's somewhere in-between. There have been a couple of projects leading up to this. There was the *De Lama Lamina* project in Brazil and in a certain respect *Drawing Restraint 9* in Japan, although that was more of a cinematic project, it was made in a very real condition, on the *Nisshin Maru* whaling ship. Then to a certain extent *Guardian of the Veil* in Manchester. I think those were all filmed situations that ended up being hybrid in their cinematic nature. I think with *Ancient Evenings* I've figured out a way to be more engaged.

HUO | First there was *Cremaster*, then you lost interest in the movie and then *Evenings* was something that can't be repeated, that can't be rehearsed, but it always produced a film as a side effect and that film charged your new interest in film. How would you describe this period, I mean everything from *Guardian of the Veil* to Detroit and eventually now the last chapter in New York? Does this chapter have a name?

MB | Well, no, it hasn't. *The Ancient Evenings* project has a name, but they are all related, that's for sure. I guess I couldn't put it more clearly than I just did in terms of this notion of ritual. I think the ritual is always there, it's always been an interest of mine and I think that the *Cremaster* works had that, but those rituals were only witnessed by those making them.

HUO | It is a witnessed ritual. Maybe it doesn't need to have name. So *Drawing Restraint* continues: where does it now stand? We did *Volume 5* for the Serpentine and now a new volume is out. What has happened since then, since 2007?

MB | Well, I did numbers *17* and *18* in Basel last year. *18* was a trampoline piece, drawing on the wall essentially, but it was a way of providing an altarpiece for an exhibition plan that was based on religious architecture. The exhibition was designed by the curator [Neville Wakefield] around the plan of a cathedral. *Drawing Restraint 17* was a longer piece, it was a two-channel video, which was based loosely on one of the Baldung Grien paintings in the exhibition, one of the *Death and the Maiden* paintings and it was presented on the façade of the museum. It was interesting to present the *Drawing Restraints* next to the passion and this religious iconography that Neville Wakefield intended. Though I think we both felt it was necessary to break up this religious reading with a non-religious connection to those Baldung paintings, those so-called memento mori paintings that were made around the same time. *Drawing Restraint 17* is something of a memento mori in that way: it follows the path of this young woman from Rudolf Steiner's Goetheanum outside of Basel to the art institution. On the "maiden" channel you see her dig a hole outside the Goetheanum, she takes a tram, along the way she takes off layers of her clothing, she meets a boy, they have a brief moment of attraction and connection and then she proceeds into the art institution. On the other channel, effectively the "death" channel, you have an artist in the Schaulager constructing a sculpture together with the art-handling team. The piece is installed and in the process part of it is broken. That night the conservator comes out, repairs the piece, and she covers the piece for the night. The maiden enters the space. She climbs the wall and ascends to the top of the institution, she reaches for the last handhold, it breaks from the wall and she falls to her death through the sculpture.

HUO | Death in the museum. Picabia said, "Museums are cemeteries!"

MB | [*laughs*] Yes! It's a simple piece but it was important for me to make an intervention with the curatorial program.

HUO | Was a stuntwoman involved?

MB | Yes, there was a stunt double doing the fall and the Maiden was performed by Emily Harrington, who is a world-class climber.

HUO | In the Serpentine piece you had a climbing wall.

MB | Yes, I've done a lot of the climbing myself in the past, so it was interesting to replace myself in that way, in that situation, with a young woman.

HUO | How does the accompanying book operate?

MB | The book has no language in it, it feels somewhat fairy-tale-like. It follows the narrative in a visual layout.

HUO | The question of the archive is also really interesting to me in terms of *Drawing Restraints*. It's very rare that a museum finds a way to buy an artist's archive during their lifetime. Archives are usually first bought when they are complete or almost complete. In your case MoMA and tha Laurenz Foundation/Schaulager have almost bought something that will happen in the future. That also happened with Gerhard Richter's *Atlas*. It was in Munich and every now and then he would send things down to Munich to add to it. There are very few examples of this and *Drawing Restraints* seems to be one of those exceptions. How does this work? What's in the contract? Are you going to send them things regularly? And what does this mean for you?

MB | The *Drawing Restraint* videos will automatically enter the archive as they are produced. The related sculpture is harder to define in terms of being inside or outside of the concept of the archive. We will need to take this on a case-by-case basis, which of course is a challenge with institutions of this scale.

HUO | So the drawings are not in the archive?

MB | They are. I am interested in having all of the drawing related to this project within the archive.

HUO | Another thing I definitely need to ask you about is your unrealized projects. The last time I asked you was in 2009.

MB | Yes, they're starting to stack up! OK, so here's an unrealized project. I was planning to perform one of the *Ancient Evenings* acts in Norman Mailer's brownstone in Brooklyn.

HUO | Was this before or after his death?

MB | After. He wrote many of his books there, it's an interesting place. He gutted the whole top of the space and made these ladders, plankways and platforms, where he would climb up every day and write in these little alcoves with views out onto the harbor. My plan was to shoot a scene in Hemmingway's house in Idaho, the house where he killed himself, and to present that scene in Mailer's apartment in the *Ka* performance in New York. The *Ka* is the manifestation of the double, of the deceased person. About two months ago, the Mailer estate put the apartment on the market, so the brownstone is being sold! I don't know if it's been sold yet, but I think this will soon become an unrealizable project. It would have been an interesting situation to perform in a domestic interior, with the chamber ensemble, on a very small scale and with an audience of about 50 people. We will try to find a way to resurrect this scene.

HUO | So his books are there?

MB | All of his books are there, a lot of his photographs and his collection of objects and paintings.

HUO | Any other unrealized or unrealizable projects?

MB | My studio is on the East River in New York and it's not far from Newtown Creek. Newtown Creek is a canal that divides Brooklyn from Queens and where the first oil refinery in the United States was built. Around a hundred years ago the Standard Oil Refinery had a massive oil spill, they say that more oil was spilled there than in the Exxon Valdez disaster. So that oil is now underneath my neighborhood in Queens and beneath the Newtown Creek. For example, they say that at the bottom of Newtown Creek there's 15 feet of black mayonnaise, which they can't really remove. To move it would agitate it and make it more toxic. They are trying to figure out how to get rid of it, but it's just there. So I was interested in making a necropolis in my studio, making a subterranean architecture, by cutting through the floor, opening up rooms and corridors and chambers.

HUO | To see the oil?

MB | The oil is of interest to me of course, but the reality is that it's completely toxic, and to put people in that environment is irresponsible. So we dug a hole in the studio until we hit the river and sure enough, oil started leeching out of the earth and into the water and there was a scum of oil on the surface of the water immediately. It smelled like opening up a bottle of solvent or something, it was unbelievable. We took a soil sample and sent it off for analysis and it came back as being volatile and unsafe, so I will not be able to make that scene in the studio. I was very interested in performing it in that environment: leaving my studio as it is and creating a situation beneath the floor that would be like a mud environment. As the tide changes the water would have to be pumped out continuously. I was planning to take this salt water that was removed and create a system of evaporation pools so that the salt could be taken out of the water and natron beds would then be used as the scene to embalm the protagonist. Another unrealized project.

HUO | One last question. Rainer Maria Rilke wrote a lovely book decades ago, which is advice to a young poet. What is your advice to a young artist in 2011?

MB | I would say that making art is like quitting smoking. If you do not have 100% conviction it will never happen.

Matthew Barney

Born in San Francisco in 1967. Matthew Barney's artistic career began with the staging of performance pieces inside the athletic facilities of Yale University while a student there in the late 1980s. Within a few years of graduating he secured shows at the San Francisco Museum of Modern Art, Documenta IX, the Whitney Biennial and the Venice Biennial and by the end of the 1990s he had become one of the most renowned artists alive, his cinematic *Cremaster* series exerting influence far beyond the bounds of the art world. Making use of a wide and expanding spectrum of media and platforms, Barney creates a world within our world, a complex and self-referential web of historical narratives and artifacts drawing on a diverse semantic pallete. He has exhibited all around the world, including a major retrospective of the *Cremaster* cycle organized by the Solomon R. Guggenheim Museum, New York and also shown at Museum Ludwig in Cologne and Musée d'Art Moderne de la Ville de Paris (2002–03) and solo exhibitions at Astrup Fearnley Museet for Moderne Kunst in Oslo (2003), Living Art Museum in Reykjavik (2003), 21st Century Museum of Contemporary Art in Kanazawa (2005), Sammlung-Goetz in Munich (2007), Fondazione Merz in Turin (2008), Schaulager in Basel (2010) as well as receiving numerous prizes, including the "Europa 2000" prize at the XLV Venice Biennale; the Hugo Boss Prize; the Glen Dimplex Award; and the Kaiser Ring Award. Matthew Barney lives and works in New York City.

Hans Ulrich Obrist

Born in Zurich in 1968. Since 2006 he has served as Co-Director of Exhibitions and Programmes and Director of International Projects at the Serpentine Gallery in London, where he currently lives and works. From 1991 to the present, he has curated over 200 exhibitions in various fields of contemporary art. In addition to these projects, he is the editor of a series of artist books published by Verlag der Buchhandlung Walther König.

Acknowledgements (in alphabetical order)

Herbert Abrell
Michael Amzalag
Tom Ashforth
Mathias Augustyniak
Agnes b
Mike Bellon
Klaus Biesenbach
Björk
Laurence Bossé
Sadie Coles
Barbara Gladstone
Koo Jeong-A
André Korbmacher
Bettina Korek
Franz König
Walther König
Sarah Lucas
Caroline Luce
Philippe Parreno
Jo Paton
Julia Peyton-Jones
Alex Poots
Kathryn Rattee
Nancy Spector
Allyson Spellacy
Anna Lena Vaney
Lorraine Two

The Conversation Series

The Conversation Series 1
Robert Crumb.
Hans Ulrich Obrist.
ISBN 978-3-88375-948-7
€ 9.80 / chf 18.50

The Conversation Series 2
John Chamberlain.
Hans Ulrich Obrist.
ISBN 978-3-88375-922-7
€ 12.80 / chf 24.–

The Conversation Series 3
Konrad Klapheck.
Hans Ulrich Obrist.
Hans-Peter Feldmann.
ISBN 978-3-86560-035-6
€ 12.80 / chf 24.–

The Conversation Series 4
Rem Koolhaas.
Hans Ulrich Obrist.
ISBN 978-3-86560-077-6
€ 9.80 / chf 18.50

The Conversation Series 6
Wolfgang Tillmans.
Hans Ulrich Obrist.
ISBN 978-3-86560-133-9
€ 14.80 / chf 27.50

The Conversation Series 7
Yona Friedman.
Hans Ulrich Obrist.
ISBN 978-3-86560-171-1
€ 14.80 / chf 27.50

The Conversation Series 8
Zaha Hadid.
Hans Ulrich Obrist.
ISBN 978-3-86560-078-3
€ 14.80 / chf 27.50

The Conversation Series 9
Gilbert & George.
Hans Ulrich Obrist.
ISBN 978-3-86560-217-6
€ 16.80 / chf 31.–

The Conversation Series 10
Thomas Demand.
Hans Ulrich Obrist.
ISBN 978-3-86560-204-6
€ 16.80 / chf 31.–

The Conversation Series 11
Nancy Spero.
Hans Ulrich Obrist.
ISBN 978-3-86560-322-7
€ 14.80 / chf 27.50

The Conversation Series 12
Dominique Gonzalez-Foerster.
Hans Ulrich Obrist.
ISBN 978-3-86560-334-0
€ 14.80 / chf 27.50

The Conversation Series 13
Olafur Eliasson.
Hans Ulrich Obrist.
ISBN 978-3-86560-335-7
€ 16.80 / chf 31.–

The Conversation Series 14
Philippe Parreno.
Hans Ulrich Obrist.
ISBN 978-3-86560-340-1
€ 14.80 / chf 27.50

The Conversation Series 15
Enzo Mari.
Hans Ulrich Obrist.
ISBN 978-3-86560-401-9
€ 12.80 / chf 24.–

The Conversation Series 16
Gustav Metzger.
Hans Ulrich Obrist.
ISBN 978-3-86560-498-9
€ 14.80 / chf 27.50

The Conversation Series 17
Yoko Ono.
Hans Ulrich Obrist.
ISBN 978-3-86560-652-5
€ 14.80 / chf 27.50

The Conversation Series 18
John Baldessari.
Hans Ulrich Obrist.
ISBN 978-3-86560-500-9
€ 12.80 / chf 24.–

The Conversation Series 19
Christian Boltanski.
Hans Ulrich Obrist.
ISBN 978-3-86560-513-9
€ 19.80 / chf 35.90

The Conversation Series 20
Rirkrit Tiravanija.
Hans Ulrich Obrist.
ISBN 978-3-86560-654-9
€ 16.80 / chf 31.–

The Conversation Series 21
Cedric Price.
Hans Ulrich Obrist.
ISBN 978-3-86560-093-6
€ 19.80 / chf 35.90

The Conversation Series 22
Jeff Koons.
Hans Ulrich Obrist.
ISBN 978-3-86560-635-8
€ 16.80 / chf 31.–

The Conversation Series 23
Marina Abramović.
Hans Ulrich Obrist.
ISBN 978-3-86560-475-0
€ 19.80 / chf 35.90

The Conversation Series 24
Cerith Wyn Evans.
Hans Ulrich Obrist.
ISBN 978-3-86560-633-4
€ 19.80 / chf 35.90

The Conversation Series 25
Dan Graham.
Hans Ulrich Obrist.
ISBN 978-3-86560-791-1
€ 16.80 / chf 31.–

The Conversation Series 26
Kazuyo Sejima & Ryue Nishizawa.
Hans Ulrich Obrist.
ISBN 978-3-86560-927-4
€ 16.80 / chf 31.–

The Conversation Series 27
Matthew Barney.
Hans Ulrich Obrist.
ISBN 978-3-86335-199-1
€ 16.80 / chf 31.–

The Conversation Series 28
Tacita Dean.
Hans Ulrich Obrist.
ISBN 978-3-86335-262-2
€ 16.80 / chf 31.–

Copy Editor
Tom Ashforth

Design
André Korbmacher, Cologne

Production
DZA Druckerei zu Altenburg GmbH, Altenburg

Photos by:
Cover: Ari Marcopoulos
pp. 25 and 64 Chris Winget
p. 86 David Regen
pp. 98, 107, 112, 133 and 142 Hugo Glendinning
p. 136 Chris Seguine

Published by
Verlag der Buchhandlung Walther König, Köln
Ehrenstr. 4, 50672 Cologne
Tel. + 49 221 20 59 6-53
E-mail: verlag@buchhandlung-walther-koenig.de

The Deutsche Nationalbibliothek lists this publication in the Deutsche Nationalbibliografie; detailed bibliographic data are available on the Internet at http://dnb.d-nb.de.

Printed in Germany

Outside Europe:
D.A.P. / Distributed Art Publishers, Inc.
155 6th Avenue, 2nd Floor
USA-New York, NY 10013
Tel. +1 800 338-BOOK; Fax: +1 212 627-9484
www.artbook.com

ISBN 978-3-86335-199-1